The Quotable Walker

The Quotable Walker

BY THE EDITORS OF
WALKING MAGAZINE

THE LYONS PRESS

Designed by Compset, Inc.

Printed in the United States of America

10 9 8 7 6 5 4 3 2 1

Library of Congress Cataloging-in-Publication Data

The quotable walker / by the editors of Walking magazine.
   p. cm.
Includes index.
ISBN 1-58574-167-1
   1. Walking—Quotations, maxims, etc. I. Walking (Boston, Mass.)

PN6084.W32 Q68 2000
796.51—dc21   00-057178

Contents

Acknowledgments

This may look like a small book, but it took a large cast of dedicated individuals (and walkers) to make it happen. Linda Frahm, *Walking Magazine* editor, spearheaded the project. Tim Lane from Des Moines, Iowa, served as its primary researcher. *Walking Magazine* staff who worked on the project included: Seth Bauer, editor-in-chief, Ericka Kostka, associate editor, and Lori Lundberg, assistant managing editor. Barbara Bowen served as the book's agent; Becky Koh from Lyon's Press was its inspiration and editor. And a special thanks goes to *Walking* interns from various colleges who spent countless hours on this book: Catherine Croteau, Amy Dunaway, Donna Fennessy, Eva Kaye, Julia Maranan, and Amanda Span.

The Body

Walking isn't just transportation: it's a chance to learn what your body can do, and to feel what exercise does for your body. Throughout history, walking has been seen as the best route to stamina and longevity. "I have two doctors," said George Macaulay Trevelyan, "My left leg and my right." For many modern walkers, walking represents the connection between the work our bodies were designed to do and the leisure we have created for ourselves through our own cleverness. But, as these quotes reveal, not everyone can get where they're trying to go. Some address physical limitations with humor, others with determination. As paralyzed football player Mike Utley insists, "I'm either gonna walk or die trying." When you think of the physical return of walking, you're obliged to remember that mobility is a gift.

If I'd known I was going to live this long, I'd have taken better care of myself."

EUBIE BLAKE

"You have to stay in shape. My grandmother, she started walking five miles a day when she was sixty. She's ninety-seven today and we don't know where the hell she is."

ELLEN DEGENERES

"A woman is as young as her knees."

MARY QUANT
"UNCOMMON SCOLD"

"And perhaps even for learning to walk in worn-out shoes, it is as well to have dry, warm feet when we are children."

NATALIA GINZBURG
"WORN-OUT SHOES" TRANSLATED BY ROBERT LOWELL

———•··•———

"Black women's faces usually hold up really, really well. But the bodies tend to go. In the past black women have not worked out as much as white women. My mother and grandmother didn't start taking care of their bodies at a young age. I've been working hard at this since my twenty-fifth birthday. So my fetish is to keep my body in shape so I can work for a long, long time."

LELA ROCHON, ACTRESS

"We have had people to stay who refuse to believe that walking can be hard exercise. It's not a dramatic effort, not immediately punishing, not fast, not violent. Everybody walks, they say. You can't call that exercise. Eventually, if they insist, we take them out for a stroll with the dogs. . . They will never again dismiss walking as nonexercise."

PETER MAYLE
TOUJOURS PROVENCE

"I'm the walkingest girl around. I like to work at it—really get my heart pounding. Sometimes [my boyfriend and I will] start out thinking we're going to catch a cab on the next block, but we bypass the cab and walk to our destination."

AMY YASBECK,
COSTAR OF TV'S *WINGS*

"The energy generated by simply putting one foot in front of the other buffered the pain enough that I could begin to examine it, to hold it for a while without flinching."

MARY H. FRAKES
MINDWALKS

"Your body is built for walking."

GARY YANKER
GARY YANKER'S WALKING WORKOUTS

"I love to walk, and when I'm in New York will cover forty to fifty blocks at a time. In Hong Kong, I live in an apartment on the fifth floor. Rather than take the elevator, I walk up the stairs. Those little exercises constantly keep the body on the alert."

MICHELLE YEOH, ACTRESS

"I dream of hiking into my old age. I want to be able even then to pack my load and take off slowly but steadily along the trail."

MARLYN S. DOAN
HIKING LIGHT

"[Hiking] is the best workout! It trims your glutes and calves and defines your legs. You can hike for three hours and not even realize you're working out. And, hiking alone lets me have some time to myself. . . Being thin shouldn't be the goal. The goal should be being healthy and strong in mind, body, and spirit. That comes from having a healthy outlook on exercise and on life in general. I think that's been lost, because everyone wants the quick fix.

JAMIE LUNER,
COSTAR OF NBC-TV'S *PROFILER* (*SHAPE MAGAZINE*)

"His attitude is, 'I'm either gonna walk or die trying.'"

PERSONAL TRAINER BLAIR MCHANEY ON MIKE UTLEY,
PARALYZED NFL STAR DETERMINED TO WALK AGAIN

"He who limps is still walking."

STANISLAW J. LEC

"An object at rest tends to stay at rest and an object in motion tends to stay in motion with the same speed and in the same direction unless acted upon by an unbalanced force."

SIR ISAAC NEWTON
NEWTON'S LAWS OF MOTION

"As a nation we are dedicated to keeping physically fit—and parking as close to the stadium as possible."

BILL VAUGHAN
THE BATHROOM SPORTS ALMANAC

"If humans were meant to walk, they'd stand up-right, have two legs, and opposable thumbs."

MARK FENTON, *WALKING MAGAZINE'S* EDITOR AT LARGE, MAKING LIGHT OF ARGUMENTS THAT WALKING IS ANYTHING LESS THAN HUMANKIND'S MOST NATURAL EXERCISE ACTIVITY.

"To put it politely as possible, America, take a walk."

VICE PRESIDENT AL GORE, AT THE PRESS CONFERENCE ANNOUNCING THE SURGEON GENERAL'S RECOMMENDATION THAT ALL AMERICANS GET AT LEAST THIRTY MINUTES OF ACTIVITY MOST DAYS OF THE WEEK.

"Taste your legs, sir: put them into motion."

WILLIAM SHAKESPEARE
SIR TOBY BELCH, *TWELFTH NIGHT*, ACT III, SCENE 1

———•••••———

"Nature has provided us with precisely the equip-
ment that furnishes to *every one* the possibility of the
right kind of exercise . . . in other words, *walking*."

EDWARD PAYSON WESTON
TO REPORTERS IN 1967

———•••••———

"Two kinds of feet exist. Every army knows this but
won't admit it for fear of losing recruits. You may be
tall, handsome, intelligent, graceful, and gifted, but
if you have feet of despair you might just as well be
a dwarf who shines shoes on the Via del Corso. Feet
of despair are too tender, and can't fight back."

MARK HELPRIN
A SOLDIER OF THE GREAT WAR

"Make your feet your friend."

J. M. BARRIE
SENTIMENTAL TOMMY

"I first became aware of a negative feeling I had about toes as a private in the army in Fort Bragg, North Carolina. We were asked . . . 'asked' is not exactly the word . . . to make a twenty-five-mile march with full packs. By the end of ten miles I was aware of my toes. I knew, without looking, that they were rubbed raw. At the fifteen-mile mark, I couldn't think of anything by my toes. By the time we reached our destination, I hated my toes as much as I hated Sgt. Fischuk, whose idea the twenty-five-mile march was in the first place."

ANDY ROONEY
"DOWN ON MY TOES" FROM *SWEET & SOUR*

"The wearer best knows where the shoe pinches."

IRISH PROVERB

"My feet, they haul me round the house, / They hoist me up the stairs; / I only have to steer them, and / they ride me everywheres."

GELETT BURGESS
"MY FEET"

"To walk one must use his feet."

AMERICAN PROVERB

"She raised her little skirts and displayed her little legs. She was thinking that, after all, feet are the most important part of the whole person; women, she said to herself, have been loved for their feet alone. Seeing nothing but her feet, she imagined perhaps that the rest of her body was of a piece with those beautiful feet."

VIRGINIA WOOLF
"STREET HAUNTING"

"Pooh was walking through the forest one day, humming proudly to himself. He had made up a little hum that very morning, as he was doing his Stoutness Exercises. . . It went like this:

Tra-la-la, tra-la-la,

Tra-la-la, tra-la-la,

Rum-tum-tiddle-um-tum.

Tiddle-iddle, tiddle-iddle,

Tiddle-iddle, tiddle-iddle,

Rum-tum-tum-tiddle-um."

A.A. MILNE
WINNIE THE POOH

"When you have worn out your shoes, the strength of the shoe leather has passed into the fiber of your body. I measure your health by the number of shoes and hats and clothes you have worn out."

RALPH WALDO EMERSON

"The feet, the feet were beautiful on the mountains; their toil was the price of all communication, and their reward the first service and refreshment. They were blessed and bathed; they suffered, but they were friends with the earth; dews in grass at morning, shallow rivers at noon, gave them coolness. They must have grown hard upon their mountain paths, yet never so hard but they needed and had the first pity and the readiest succour. It was never easy for the feet of man to travel this earth, shod or unshod, and his feet are delicate, like his colour."

ALICE MEYNELL
"THE FOOT"

"Here where the wind is always north-northeast/ And children learn to walk on frozen toes."

EDWIN ARLINGTON ROBINSON
"NEW ENGLAND"

—•••—

"All of us are aware that individuals walk differently; one can often recognize an acquaintance by his manner of walking even when seen at a distance. Tall, slender people walk differently from short, stocky people. . . A person walks differently when exhilarated than when mentally depressed."

BIOMECHANISTS VERNE T. INMAN, HENRY J. RALSTON, AND FRANK TODD

Companions

Who do you walk with? A lover? A stranger? A friend? Many of us are of two minds about companionship when walking. On the one hand, walking is by nature the most social of physical activities. Having someone to be with and talk to can be a source of comfort and a way to pass the time. A shared experience is often a better one—a feeling expressed by John Milton, who asks, "In solitude/What happiness?" On the other hand, walking alone allows for conversations with one's self. Those in favor of solitary walking might agree with Edward Gibson, who said, "I was never less alone than when by myself." And then there are still those of us who are simply opposed to bad companionship. As Fred Allen says, "I like long walks, especially when they are taken by people who annoy me."

"A friend I went to high school with lives next door to me, and we walk our dogs together. It's great because even if I can't get to a workout, I'm still doing forty minutes of walking."

CHRISTA MILLER,
COSTAR OF TV'S *THE DREW CAREY SHOW*

"I have three personal trainers: [my sons] Sam, John, and Joe. I'm always carrying them up and down the stairs. When I take my walks, I'm pushing a double stroller, which makes things a lot more strenuous."

PATRICIA HEATON,
CO STAR OF CBS'S *EVERYBODY LOVES RAYMOND*

"I walk with my friends and make new friends while walking."

MARLYN S. DOAN
HIKING LIGHT

"A real friend is one who walks in when the rest of the world walks out."

WALTER WINCHELL

"The true charm of pedestrians does not lie in the walking, or in the scenery, but in the talking."

MARK TWAIN
A TRAMP ABROAD

"Two great talkers will not travel far together."

GEORGE BORROW

"It's easier to find a traveling companion than to get rid of one."

PEG BRACKEN

"I cannot see the wit of walking and talking at the same time."

WILLIAM HAZLITT
ON GOING A JOURNEY

What really helps motivate me to walk are my dogs, who are my best pals. They keep you honest about walking because when it's time to go, you can't disappoint those little faces."

WENDIE MALICK,
COSTAR OF NBC'S *JUST SHOOT ME*

"Many people will walk in and out of your life, but only true friends will leave footprints in your heart."

ELEANOR ROOSEVELT

"I like long walks, especially when they are taken by people who annoy me."

FRED ALLEN

"I hadn't asked him why he wanted to come. Katz was the one person I knew on earth who might be on the run from guys with names like Julio and Mr. Big. Anyway, I didn't care. I wasn't going to have to walk alone."

BILL BRYSON
A WALK IN THE WOODS

———◆◆◆———

"In solitude
What happiness? Who can enjoy alone,
Or all enjoying, what contentment find?"

JOHN MILTON
PARADISE LOST

"Whoever undertakes a long Journey, if he be wise, makes it his Business to find out an agreeable Companion."

CERVANTES
DON QUIXOTE, II, 19

"Like one, that on a lonesome road
Doth walk in fear and dread,
And having once turned round walks on,
And turns no more his head;
Because he knows, a frightful fiend
Doth close behind him tread. . ."

SAMUEL TAYLOR COLERIDGE
"THE RIME OF THE ANCIENT MARINER"

"I can enjoy society in a room; but out of doors, nature is company enough for me."

WILLIAM HAZLITT
"ON GOING A JOURNEY"

———◆———

"Our friends go with us as we go / Down the long path where Beauty wends / Where all we love foregathers, so / Why should we fear to join our friends?"

OLIVER ST. JOHN GOGARTY
"NON DOLET"

———◆———

"We've come this far. Let's make the last step together."

JIM WICKWIRE TO LOU REICHARDT, PUTTING THEIR ARMS
AROUND EACH OTHER AND BECOMING THE FIRST AMERICANS
TO REACH THE SUMMIT OF K2 IN 1978.
"THE QUOTABLE CLIMBER"

"In a little city like Dublin one meets every person whom one knows within a few days. Around each bend in the road there is a friend, an enemy, a bore striding towards you."

JAMES STEPHENS
THE CHARWOMAN'S DAUGHTER

"Two shorten the road."

IRISH PROVERB

"The man who goes alone can start today; but he who travels with another must wait till that other is ready, and it may be a long time before they get off."

HENRY DAVID THOREAU

"Now, to be properly enjoyed, a walking tour should be gone upon alone . . . because freedom is of the essence."

ROBERT LOUIS STEVENSON

"The true male never yet walked
Who liked to listen when his mate talked."

ANNA WICKHAM

"I was never less alone than when by myself."

EDWARD GIBBON

"No road is long with good company."

ALFRED VICTOR VIGNY

"He who has travelled alone can tell what he likes."

RWANDAN PROVERB

"Lady, will you walk about with your friend?"

DON PEDRO,
MUCH ADO ABOUT NOTHING, ACT II, SCENE I

"Let none disturb us.—Why should
this change of thoughts,
The sad companion, dull-eyed melancholy,
Be my so used a guest as not an hour,
In the day's glorious walk, or peaceful night...."

WILLIAM SHAKESPEARE
PERICLES, *PERICLES, PRINCE OF TYRE*, ACT I, SCENE II

"I drew my bride, beneath the moon,
Across my threshold; happy hour!
But, ah, the walk that afternoon
We saw the water-flags in flower!"

COVENTRY PATMORE

"If I had to choose between him and a cockroach as
a companion for a walking-tour, the cockroach
would have had it by a short head."

P. G. WODEHOUSE
MY MAN JEEVES

"Walking together for so many years/ They could hold hand in hand and still avoid / What a jackhapper or a dog had done / To or on the sidewalk-such was the supple / Touch they kept in, such the ample closeness / That marked their every way of walking by / The way (and sitting in their house and lying / Down and rising up, for all that, as well)"

JOHN HOLLANDER
"BREAD-AND-BUTTER!" FROM TESSERAE

———

"Can two walk together, except they be agreed?"

AMOS 3:3

———

"I'd rather one should walk with me than merely tell the way."

EDGAR ALBERT GUEST
"SERMONS WE SEE"

"'O Oysters, come and walk with us!' / The Walrus did beseech. / 'A pleasant walk, a pleasant talk, / Along the briny beach.'"

LEWIS CARROLL
THE WALRUS AND THE CARPENTER

"Yea, though I walk through the valley of the shadow of death, I will fear no evil: for thou art with me."

PSALM 23

"The Cat. He walked by himself, and all places were alike to him."

RUDYARD KIPLING
THE CAT THAT WALKED BY HIMSELF

"And Enoch walked with God."

GENESIS 5:24

"I walked a mile with Pleasure. / She Chattered all the way, / But left me none the wiser / For all she had to say.

I walked a mile with Sorrow/ And ne'er a word said she; / But, oh, the things I learned from her / When Sorrow walked with me!"

ROBERT BROWNING HAMILTON
"ALONG THE ROAD"

"Forgotten mornings when he walked with his mother / Through the parables / Of sunlight"

DYLAN THOMAS
"POEM IN OCTOBER"

"Have ye not seen us walking every day? / Was there a tree about which did not know / The love betwixt us two?"

ABRAHAM COWLEY
"ON THE DEATH OF MR. WILLIAM HARVEY"

"Today I have grown taller from walking with the trees."

KARLE WILSON BAKER
"GOOD COMPANY"

"Who is the third who walks always beside you?"

T. S. ELIOT
THE WASTE LAND

"But, as usual, he walked to and fro, and during the day did not pass from out the turmoil of that street. And, as the shades of the second evening came on, I grew wearied unto death, and stopping fulling in front of the wanderer, gazed at him steadfastly in the face. He noticed me not, but resumed his solemn walk, while I, ceasing to follow, remained absorbed in contemplation."

EDGAR ALLEN POE
THE MAN OF THE CROWD

"And, in what savage spot / I chance to be, in what most barren shore, / Ever more beautiful she walks with me."

PETRARCH
"ODE 17"

"It was a very fine November day, and the Miss Musgroves came through the little grounds, and stopped for no other purpose than to say, that they were going to take a long walk, and therefore concluded Mary could not like to go with them; and when Mary immediately replied, with some jealousy at not being supposed a good walker, 'Oh, yes, I should like to join you very much, I am very fond of a long walk.' "

JANE AUSTEN
PERSUASION

"I forgot that your light foot / was transformed into ashes, / and, as during good times, / I ventured to find you / along the path."

GABRIELA MISTRAL
"THE USELESS VIGIL"

"This first bright day has broken / the back of winter. / We rise from war / to walk across the earth / around our house / both stunned that sun can shine so brightly / after all our pain"

> AUDRE LORDE
> "WALKING OUR BOUNDARIES" FROM *THE BLACK UNICORN*

"My yesterdays walk with me. They keep step, they are gray faces that peer over my shoulder."

> WILLIAM GOLDING ON THE INFLUENCE OF HIS NAVAL SERVICE DURING WORLD WAR II.

"I am yours for the walk; and especially when I walk away."

> HERO, *MUCH ADO ABOUT NOTHING*, ACT II, SCENE I

"Tell me with whom you travel and I'll tell you who you are."

ALFRED VICTOR VIGNY

Explorations

There are many ways to think about exploration. The journeys of which most of us speak are journeys into the natural world. Often, upon our return, we find we've learned more about the world around us and our place in it. As Ezra Pound says: "Learn of the green world what can be thy place." Colin Fletcher describes making discoveries about other people when he writes "I have emerged from wild country and have found myself face to face with astonished people who had obviously felt that they were already at the edge of the world." But often, the most rewarding explorations are the ones in which we discover a new part of ourselves. As George Moore writes, "A man travels the world over in search of what he needs, and returns home to find it."

"Late at night, under a full moon, there's nothing like powerwalking through the Hollywood Hills to enjoy some of my favorite old 'haunts.' I just love a fast-paced hike by Frank Lloyd Wright's Ennis-Brown house or a leisurely stroll through the Hollywood Memorial Park Cemetery—the only place in Hollywood where you're guaranteed to get within six feet of your favorite star. It's the best exercise I know to keep my ghoulish figure. Now if they just made a good walking shoe with spiked heels. . ."

ELVIRA, "MISTRESS OF THE DARK"

"The thing I love the most, that I don't need to be talked into, is hiking the trails at the end of our street that go into the Santa Monica Mountains. They're hard trails, and the vistas are unbelievable. Talk about walking with God. It's so beautiful."

VICKI LEWIS,
ACTRESS

"I love to walk down my creek bed with my dogs; I have hills and woods and fields. I love nature. My land. Terra firma, earth. I love the sky and the wind and my animals. I've come to terms that I'll never be a size eight, but I take care of myself, and that means keeping my body, my mind, and my spirit healthy."

WYNONNA JUDD

"I'd love to tell you that I walk strictly for the health benefits, really I would. But to tell you the absolute truth, I walk because I'm nosy and I like to snoop, and there's no better way to scope out what's going on in my neighborhood than to walk . . . who's moved out, who's renovating, who's landscaping. We walk the dogs in the morning and the evening, and if you're really nosy, sometimes nighttime is really good, because then everyone's lights are on and . . ."

LEILA KENZLE,
STAR OF UPN'S *DIRESTA*

"We shall not cease from exploration
And the end of all our exploring
Will be to arrive where we started
And know the place for the first time."

T.S. ELIOT
"FOUR QUARTETS"

"All of us need to keep in touch with wild, unruly things, even if we do it in the tamest possible way."

> MAGGIE NICHOLS
> *WILD, WILD WOMAN*

"For my part, I travel not to go anywhere, but to go. I travel for travel's sake. The great affair is to move."

> ROBERT LOUIS STEVENSON
> "CHEYLARD AND LUC," FROM *TRAVELS WITH A DONKEY*

"People have said, 'Build this trail and no one will come'... Now commuters use it every day and families come on weekends to blade and bike and walk."

> TOM MURPHY
> MAYOR OF PITTSBURGH, PA, SPEAKING OF THE
> ELIZA FURNACE TRAIL

"Throughout its length the A.T. and its side trails offer a feast of tempting names. Most musical are the old Indian names, like Matagamon, Kokadjo, Kennebago, Ammonoosuc, Moosilauke, Popolopen, Menomini, Amicalola, Chattahoochee.

English meanings of some are obscure. Who cares, when they sing so sweetly? Many place names along and near the Trail are simply descriptive: Sugarloaf, Saddleback, Hawksbill; Pulpit Rock, Hangover Mountain; Ice Water Spring, and Lonesome Lake . . . "

ANDREW H. BROWN
"SKYLINE TRAIL FROM MAINE TO GEORGIA," FROM
NATIONAL GEOGRAPHIC

"We have the peculiar privilege . . . the freedom to walk this earth, see its beauties, taste its sweetness, partake of its enduring strength."

HAL BORLAND

"The whole object of travel is not to set foot on foreign land; it is at last to set foot on one's own country as a foreign land."

G.K. CHESTERTON
"THE RIDDLE OF THE IVY," FROM *TREMENDOUS TRIFLES*

"Learn of the green world what can be thy place."

EZRA POUND

"A man travels the world over in search of what he needs, and returns home to find it."

GEORGE MOORE
"THE BOOK OF KERITH"

"A traveller without observation is a bird without wings."

MOSLIH EDDIN SAADI
"WISDOM OF THE AGES AT YOUR FINGERTIPS"

"Every perfect traveler always created the country where he travels."

NIKOS KAZANTZAKIS
"PEARLS OF WISDOM"

"Half the fun of the travel is the esthetic of lost-ness."

Ray Bradbury
"California"

"Is there something we have forgotten? some precious thing/ We have lost, wandering in strange lands?"

Arna Bontemps
"Nocturne at Bethesda"

"The best damn country I've ever been in."

DAVID KUNST
ON THE UNITED STATES, UPON RETURNING HOME FROM HIS
FOUR-YEAR WALK AROUND THE WORLD

"Two or three hours' walking will carry me to as strange a country as I expect ever to see."

HENRY DAVID THOREAU

"I started going for long lone country walks among the spendthrift gold and glory of the year-end, giving myself up to the earth-scents and the skywinds and all the magic of the countryside which is ordained for the healing of the soul."

MONICA BALDWIN
ON THE ENGLISH COUNTRYSIDE, *I Leap Over the Wall*

"Afoot and light-hearted I take to the open road,
Healthy, free, the world before me,
The long brown path before me leading wherever I
　　choose."

WALT WHITMAN
"THE OPEN ROAD"

"There's music in the Irish names—
Kilkenny . . . Tipperary . . .
There's beauty in the countryside,
From Cork to Londonderry,
And whoever makes his earthy home
Close to the Irish sod
Has found a bit of Heaven
And walks hand in hand with God."

IRISH BLESSING

"He and his six *amis* had come to the New World to gain *gloire* and *honneur* through *nouveaux exploits* despite *les dangers*, but instead got lost and spent June and July looking for the route back to where they had come from, the Northeast Passage."

GARRISON KEILLOR
LAKE WOBEGON DAYS

———

"Many times in recent years I have emerged from wild country, happy and whole and secure and content, and have found myself face to face with astonished people who had obviously felt that they were already at the edge of the world."

COLIN FLETCHER
THE COMPLETE WALKER III

"Nothing is so awesomely unfamiliar as the familiar that discloses itself at the end of a journey."

CYNTHIA OZICK

"There are only two rules. One is E. M. Forster's guide to Alexandria: the best way to know Alexandria is to wander aimlessly. The second is from the Psalms: grin like a dog and run about through the city."

JAN MORRIS

"The world is a book, and those who do not travel, read only a page."

SAINT AUGUSTINE

"My daughters and I learned some Spanish, shared in another family's life, walked confidently in the dark, laughed at ourselves, and ate too much ice cream. Most importantly, we returned home, forever changed, surer of ourselves, strengthened, stretched, and having touched other women with our spirits."

MARYBETH BOND
"GUARDIANS OF THE DARK"

"The Fool wanders, the wise Man travels."

THOMAS FULLER

"A man that hath traveled knoweth many things."

BOOK OF WISDOM

"Little by little, one travels far."
"All that is gold does not glitter; not all those that wander are lost."

J. R. R. TOLKIEN
THE FELLOWSHIP OF THE RING

"He that travels far knows much."

JOHN CLARKE
PAROEMIOLOGIA

"Travel and change of place impart new vigor to the mind."

SENECA

"We walked a thousand miles and the way seemed short."

KAN'AMI KIYTSUGU
"SOTOBA KOMACHI," TRANSLATED BY SAM HOUSTON BROCK

"Walking, I can almost hear the redwoods beating."

LINDA HOGAN
"WALKING"

"Do you know what solitude which is in itself satisfying? Have you traveled miles through the long white aisles of the green timber where the snow was so deep that nothing could exist without wings or snowshoes?"

SHIRLEY C. HULSE

The Mind

Walking gives the mind free rein. Inside, sitting down, thoughts tend to run in endless circles. Outside, walking, the mind can roam as the body does. The freedom of the outdoors and physical movement provide an escape from what Mary Frakes describes as "the drone" of thoughts. Through walking, she says, they are replaced with the rhythm of moving feet. As Colin Fletcher writes, walking is a way of "escaping from reality." One of the most surprising effects of walking is its ability to lead your mind to insights about yourself. As John Muir observed, "Going out, I found, was really going in." Where might your mind wander when freed from itself?

"I take a full day off from soccer each week. Instead, I walk or take a slow relaxing jog, get a massage, and stretch. . . . It's important to look forward to whatever activity you participate in. It can't be something you dread, or you won't stick with it."

MICHELLE AKERS,
MEMBER OF THE 1999 U.S. WOMEN'S WORLD CUP
CHAMPIONSHIP SOCCER TEAM

"Walking is sort of a religion to me, and though I've slowed down a bit this year, it's still my favorite cure-all. There's hardly any problem that a walk can't solve."

REBECCA WELLS,
AUTHOR OF *THE DIVINE SECRETS OF THE YA-YA SISTERHOOD*

"I work out because it's important to me. [My advice for others is to] take care of yourself, because if you're not in shape and not in a good place, you're not going to be a good mom. It doesn't matter whether it's a half-hour in the tub with a magazine or an hour-long walk."

MEL HARRIS,
COSTAR OF NBC'S *SOMETHING SO RIGHT*

"Above all, do not lose your desire to walk. Every day I walk myself into a state of well-being and walk away from every illness. I have walked myself into my best thoughts, and I know of no thought so burdensome that one cannot walk away from it . . . if one just keeps on walking, everything will be all right."

SOREN KIERKEGAARD

"I'll be up against a book deadline and I'll discover that my husband forgot to walk the dog. Or I'll come back into town, exhausted, and realize that I have to go food shopping—suddenly, grudgingly, I find myself out there walking the aisles of a farmer's market or walking the dog. Halfway through I realize that I've clamed down, that I'm actually thinking more clearly and relaxing about whatever pressures I've let build up. . . . I've written entire chapters in my mind while walking, and I always work out the words for a lecture or a speech while I'm out with the dog. There's something about the exercise, fresh air, and lack of other distractions that enables me to zero in on whatever might have been escaping me just minutes earlier."

DEBORAH MADISON,
AUTHOR AND CHEF AT SAN FRANCISCO'S FAMED VEGETARIAN
RESTAURANT, GREENS

"My husband and I flew to Hilton Head Island and met up with my family. After spending time with them, he and I started to walk to the beach. I don't think we had a particular destination in mind. We just walked on the sand, into a small neighborhood, and then back to the beach again. We covered a couple of miles, and by the end of it I was a new person. I felt like I was sane again and happy and at peace. . . . Exercise—whether it's the treadmill or StairMaster or Richard and I walking together on the weekends or in the evenings—is my single biggest stress-control technique."

NANCY O'DELL,
CO-ANCHOR OF *ACCESS HOLLYWOOD*

"When I was shooting the made-for-TV movie *Five Desperate Hours* in Vancouver, I walked the sea wall. And I miss walking as much as I did when I lived in New York. It helps me clear my head."

SHARON LAWRENCE,
COSTAR OF NBC'S *FIRED UP*

———

"How can you explain that you need to know that the trees are still there, and the hills and the sky? Anyone knows they are. How can you say it is time your pulse responded to another rhythm, the rhythm of the day and the season instead of the hour and the minute? No, you cannot explain. So you walk."

NEW YORK TIMES EDITORIAL, "THE WALK," OCTOBER 25, 1967

"They can't seem to understand my taking this walk. The burden of their ideas in regard to such a walk is the question 'What do you get out of it?' I say I am learning lots, seeing the country and the people, and they pipe up, 'But why do you want to if you don't get something out of it?' I say I'll get lots of beautiful scenery in Colorado and farther west. 'But what's the good if you don't get something out of it?' Daily the same formula is coming through. The women don't understand."

MINNIE HILL WOOD
ON THE PEOPLE OF INDIANA AND ILLINOIS DURING HER WALK
ACROSS THE COUNTRY IN 1916 FROM WASHINGTON, DC TO
SAN FRANCISCO

"[We] live with our heels as well as head and most of our pleasure comes in that way."

JOHN MUIR
TO YOSEMITE AND BEYOND

"I think that I cannot preserve my health and spirits, unless I spend four hours a day at least—and it is commonly more than that—sauntering through the woods and over the hills and fields, absolutely free from all worldly engagements."

HENRY DAVID THOREAU

"The soul of a journey is liberty, perfect liberty, to think, feel, do, just as one pleases."

WILLIAM HAZLITT
"ON GOING A JOURNEY," *TABLE TALK*

"We live in a fast-paced society. Walking slows us down."

ROBERT SWEETGALL
FITNESS WALKING

"In search of ideas I spent yesterday morning in walking about, and went to the stores and bought things in four departments. A wonderful and delightful way of spending time. I think this sort of activity does stimulate creative ideas."

ARNOLD BENNETT
THE JOURNALS, 1911–1921

"Albert Einstein, who discovered that a tiny amount of mass is equal to a huge amount of energy, which explains why, as Einstein himself so eloquently put it in a famous 1939 speech to the Physics Department at Princeton, 'You have to exercise for a week to work off the thigh fat from a single Snickers.'"

DAVE BARRY
DAVE BARRY TURNS 50

"Solvitur ambulando, St. Jerome was fond of saying.
To solve a problem, walk around."

GREGORY MCNAMEE
"WALKING"

—————

"Now shall I walk
or shall I ride?
'Ride,' Pleasure said:
'Walk,' Joy replied."

W.H. DAVIES

—————

"Most of us are still related to our native fields as
the navigator to undiscovered islands in the sea. We
can any afternoon discover a new fruit there which
will surprise us by its beauty or sweetness."

HENRY DAVID THOREAU
WILD FRUITS

"Pray, walk awhile."

WILLIAM SHAKESPEARE
QUEEN, *CYMBELINE*, ACT I, SCENE I

"I am a *walkaholic*. . . . Walking is far too pleasurable for me to bother keeping track of the distance . . ."

BILL GALE
EMMY AWARD WINNER FOR THE DOCUMENTARY,
"HOW AMERICA STAYS PHYSICALLY FIT"

"I go mainly for exercise and often walk with my mind folded into itself and therefore cut off; but the woods are always there, calming or stimulating me according to their mood and mine."

COLIN FLETCHER
THE SECRET WORLD OF COLIN FLETCHER

"For the human spirit needs places where nature has not been rearranged by the hand of man."

ANONYMOUS

———•◆•◆•———

"I've always felt that walking was one of the best and easiest forms of physical activity available. But that was before I spent time walking on the Appalachian Trail. Now I know walking is the best mental and physical activity that exists."

CINDY PORTEOUS
NATIONAL ASSOCIATION OF GOVERNOR'S COUNCILS ON
PHYSICAL FITNESS AND SPORTS

"Hiking can bring joy to people of all ages because there are no rules about what the activity has to be like. It can match the mood and season of your life, or it can suit the mood or season of the year."

MARLYN S. DOAN
HIKING LIGHT

"the walk liberating, I was released from forms, from the perpendiculars,
    straight lines, blocks, boxes, binds
of thought / into the hues, shadings, rises, flowing
    bends and blends of sight"

A. R. AMMONS
"CORSONS INLET" FROM *COLLECTED POEMS 1951–1971*

"I have two luxuries to brood over in my walks, your loveliness and the hour of my death."

JOHN KEATS
"TO FANNY BRAWNE"

"Better! A rare strong, hearty, healthy walk—four statute miles an hour—preferable to that rumbling, tumbling, jolting, shaking, scraping, creaking, villainous old gig? Why, the two things will not admit of comparison. It is an insult to the walk, to set them side by side. Where is an instance of a gig having ever circulated a man's blood. . . . When did a gig ever sharpen anybody's wits and energies . . . ?"

CHARLES DICKENS
MARTIN CHUZZLEWIT

"'What are you doing out?'
'Walking,' said Leonard Mead.
'Walking!'
'Just walking,' he said simply, but his face felt cold.
'Walking, just walking, walking?'
'Yes, sir.'
'Walking where? For what?'
'Walking for air, Walking to *see*.'"

RAY BRADBURY
"THE PEDESTRIAN" (A CONVERSATION BETWEEN LEONARD
MEAD AND AN OFFICER IN A POLICE CAR)

"If you can't find your inspiration by walking around the block one time, go around two blocks— but never three."

ROBERT MOTHERWELL
NIGHTLINE ABC TV AUGUST 9, 1985

"Socrates: My dear Phaedrus, whence come you, and whither are you going?

Phaedrus: I come from Lysias the son of Cephalus, and I am going to take a walk outside the wall, for I have been sitting with him the whole morning; and our common friend Acumenus tells me that it is much more refreshing to walk in the open air than to be shut up in a cloister."

PLATO
"PHAEDRUS," TRANSLATED BY BENJAMIN JOWETT

"Having, then, formed the project of describing the habitual state of my soul in the strongest position in which a mortal could ever find himself, I saw no simpler and surer way to carry out this enterprise than to keep a faithful record of my solitary walks and of the reveries which fill them when I leave my head entirely free and let my ideas follow their bent without resistance or constraint."

JEAN-JACQUES ROUSSEAU
REVERIES OF THE SOLITARY WALKER

"Far from the world I walk, and from all care."

WILLIAM WORDSWORTH
"RESOLUTION"

"When you recognize with more than usual significance that your strength is greater than your need to accomplish effortlessly the swiftest of changes and to cope with it, when in this frame of mind you go striding down the long streets—then for that evening you have completely got away from your family, which fades into insubstantiality, while you yourself, a firm, boldly drawn black figure, slapping yourself on the thigh, grow to your true stature."

FRANZ KAFKA
"THE SUDDEN WALK," TRANSLATED BY WILLA AND
EDWIN MUIR

"It's my lunch hour, so I go / for a walk among the hum-colored / cabs."

FRANK O'HARA
"A STEP AWAY FROM THEM" FROM LUNCH POEMS

"There are some good things today about walking. Not many, but some. Walking takes longer, for example, than any other known form of locomotion except crawling. Thus it stretches time and prolongs life. Life is already too short to waste on speed."

EDWARD ABBEY
"WALKING"

"Some years ago, a temporary inability to sleep, referable to a distressing impression, caused me to walk about the streets all night, for a series of several nights."

CHARLES DICKENS
"NIGHT WALKS"

"Through no deliberate intention of our own, we also take more exercise. Not the grim contortions promoted by gaunt women in leotards, but the exercise that comes naturally from living in a climate that allows you to spend eight or nine months of the year outdoors. Discipline has nothing to do with it, apart from the small disciplines of country life—bringing logs in for the fire, keeping the weeds down and the ditches clear, planting, pruning, bending, and lifting. And, every day in every kind of weather, walking."

PETER MAYLE
TOUJOURS PROVENCE

"Walking revitalizes me. After one day on the trail I become different from the way I am at home. I am in touch with the seasons, the weather, the varied hours of each day. I see more keenly. I am aware of the details."

MARLYN S. DOAN
HIKING LIGHT

"I had better admit right away that walking can in the end become an addiction . . . even in this final stage it remains a delectable madness, very good for sanity, and I recommend it with passion."

COLIN FLETCHER
THE COMPLETE WALKER III

"I stroll along serenely, with my eyes, my shoes, /
my rage, forgetting everything."

PABLO NERUDA
"WALKING AROUND," TRANSLATED BY ROBERT BLY

"When we have paced the length of the beach, it is
pleasant, and not unprofitable, to retrace our steps,
and recall the whole mood and occupation of the
mind during the former passage. Our tracks, being
all discernible, will guide us with an observing con-
sciousness through every unconscious wandering of
thought and fancy. Here we followed the surf in its
reflux, to pick up a shell which the sea seemed loath
to relinquish."

NATHANIEL HAWTHORNE
"FOOT-PRINTS ON THE SEA-SHORE"

Observations

If it affords the chance to look within, walking (or the very idea of it) also induces us to look around and observe, both literally and metaphorically. Observations about walking range from the historical to the sociological to the sarcastic, such as Lyndon B. Johnson's remark, "If one morning I walked on top of the water across the Potomac River, the headline that afternoon would read: PRESIDENT CAN'T SWIM." These observations place walking in its context as a rich part of the human experience.

"Sometimes the steps themselves are very simple. In *Mozartiana*, for several measures, the ballerina just walks. In *Serenade* the dancers move their feet into first position. Ordinary steps, but in their combinations, in their relation to the music, they always connect to our emotions, they always surprise."

PETER MARTINS
PREFACE TO *TRIBUTES: CELEBRATING FIFTY YEARS OF NEW YORK BALLET*

"We've all heard of that future, and it sounds pretty lonely. In the next century, the line of thinking goes, everyone will work at home, shop at home, watch movies at home and communicate with all their friends through videophones and e-mail. It's as if science and culture have progressed for one purpose only: to keep us from ever having to get out of our pajamas."

SAN FRANCISCO CHRONICLE

"I think that the time one spends musing takes place in a kind of meadowlands of the imagination, a part of the imagination that has not yet been plowed, developed, or put to any immediate practical use. Environmentalists are always arguing that those butterflies, those grasslands, those watershed woodlands have an utterly necessary function in the grand scheme of things, even if they don't produce a market crop. The same is true of the meadowlands of the imagination. The fight for free space—for wilderness and for public space—should be accompanied by a fight for free time to spend in that space, wandering, for it is in this wandering afoot that one best reaches the wildlands of the imagination."

REBECCA SOLNIT
WANDERLUST, A HISTORY OF WALKING

"Golf is a good walk spoiled."

MARK TWAIN

"As I walked along the shoreline, I thought about how nature overwhelms everything with the sea's pastel-painted fish and purple coral, the island's extravagant trees of sweet unrecognizable fruit growing amidst waterfalls and volcanic mountains, rugged and wet. It would be difficult not to be delirious in such a place, a place where nature over-powers people, where people give themselves over to the land and sea."

LAURIE GOUGH
"LIGHT ON A MOONLESS NIGHT"

"I have met with but one or two persons in the course of my life who understood the art of Walking, that is, of taking walks—who had a genius, so to speak, for sauntering, which word is beautifully derived "from idle people who roved about the country, in the Middle Ages, and asked charity, under pretense of going la Sainte Terre," to the Holy Land, till the children exclaimed, "There goes a Sainte-Terrer," a Saunterer,—a Holy-Lander. . . . For every walk is a sort of crusade, preached by some Peter the Hermit in us, to go forth and reconquer this Holy Land from the hands of the Infidels. . . . So we saunter toward the Holy Land, till one day the sun shall shine more brightly than ever he has done, shall perchance shine into our minds and hearts, and light up our whole lives with a great awakening light, as warm and serene and golden as on a bankside in autumn."

HENRY DAVID THOREAU
Walking

"Too many programs out there are full of do's and don'ts and are very structured. The more you realize you have a choice, the more you'll feel a sense of freedom about it. Everybody needs to find a passion. That's the great thing about walking—it just clicks with so many people."

KATHY SMITH
ON HER BOOK, *GETTING BETTER ALL THE TIME*

"One drizzly day, my dog and I ended up hiking for seven hours. I'll tell you, we both slept for two days after that . . . When [my son] is with [my husband and me], there's a lot of stopping to look at things and to throw rocks. Then he gets tired and I put him on my shoulders, and I think wow, this is what it was like when I was carrying thirty extra pounds on me."

JUDI EVANS LUCIANO
COSTAR OF NBC'S *ANOTHER WORLD*

"A conservative is a man with two perfectly good legs who, however, has never learned how to walk forward."

FRANKLIN DELANO ROOSEVELT

———•••——

"If one morning I walked on top of the water across the Potomac River, the headline that afternoon would read: PRESIDENT CAN'T SWIM."

LYNDON B. JOHNSON

———•••——

"Until you walk a mile in another man's moccasins, you can't imagine the smell."

ROBERT BYRNE

"Every habit and faculty is preserved and increased by correspondent actions . . . as the habit of walking, by walking; of running by running."

EPICTETUS

"Two things militate against pleasurable walking in the country. First there is nothing to look at but trees and grass and an occasional cow . . . Second, the people who live in the country firmly believe that anybody who walks in the country is either too poor to own a car, or has just had a flat tire and is employing a secondary and highly undesirable means of locomotion to obtain help for his damaged vehicle."

JEROME WEIDMAN
BACK TALK

"Walking is a human habit into which dogs readily fall but it is a distasteful form of exercise to a cat unless he has a purpose in view."

CARL VAN VECHTEN

"And as I turn me home,
My shadow walks before."

ROBERT BRIDGES

"Man is not man sitting down; he is man on the move."

STEVEN GRAHAM
THE GENTLE ART OF TRAMPING

"No feat of strength and endurance has ever attracted so much attention in this or any other country and the 'pluck' of the young pedestrian is every where admired."

EDWARD PAYSON WESTON
HARPER'S WEEKLY 1867, ON HIS WALK FROM PORTLAND,
MAINE TO CHICAGO, ILLINOIS, ON A WAGER OF $10,000 THAT
HE WOULD ACCOMPLISH THE DISTANCE, 1,237 8/4 MILES IN 26
SECULAR DAYS—30 DAYS IN ALL.

"The whole nation turned out to be amazingly, gratifyingly friendly . . . some rather extraordinary people do exist out there."

GARRY MOORE
CALIFORNIA WRITER WHO WALKED FROM BOSTON TO
SAN DIEGO

"The people here [in Burlington, Colorado] never walk the roads outside of the towns. They either ride, or drive. For several days I haven't seen a person on foot."

MINNIE HILL WOOD
ON HER 1916 WALK FROM WASHINGTON D.C. TO SAN FRANCISCO TO PROVE THAT A LONE WOMAN COULD SAFELY WALK EVERY STEP OF THE WAY ACROSS THE UNITED STATES

"We spend the first twelve months of our children's lives teaching them to walk and talk and the next twelve telling them to sit down and shut up."

PHYLLIS DILLER

"You've seen these people who are using the Stair-Master. Have we turned into gerbils, ladies and gentlemen?"

DENIS LEARY
EXERCISE DAILY, EAT WISELY, DIE ANYWAY

———•••••———

"Walkers [are] a still more ancient and honorable class."

HENRY DAVID THOREAU

———•••••———

"As part of the Eunoto ritual of the Masai tribe, when warriors become elders they replace their spears with walking sticks."

NATIONAL GEOGRAPHIC, SEPTEMBER 1999

"'With this triumph, the effeteness of monarchial institutions becomes more evident to many minds.'"

> HARPER'S WEEKLY, ON THE ACHIEVEMENT OF DAN O'LEARY WHO WALKED 520 MILES IN 140 HOURS

"Three things one should do every year—listen to a storyteller at a fireside, give a hand in a corn harvest field, and climb an Irish mountain."

> MICHAEL JOHN MURPHY
> MOUNTAIN YEAR

"The profligacy of the age is such that we see little children not able to walk or talk running about the streets and cursing their Maker."

> SIR BOYLE ROACHE
> DURING A DEBATE IN THE IRISH HOUSE OF COMMONS

"In this Parnassus of the prairie, the Rev. Dr. Watt was the leading citizen of his day, a cleric, scholar, poet, orator, and a man who, as someone said, 'woke up each day and wrapped greatness like a cloak around him.' On his daily constitutionals, Dr. Watt is impeded by neither mud nor livestock. Morning and evening, he sets forth on his accustomed round, prepared for magnificent and learned discourse."

GARRISON KEILLOR
LAKE WOBEGON DAYS

———

"My dog would sit there all day, he would watch me walk by, he would think to himself, *I could do that! He's not that good!*"

JERRY SEINFELD
"NO POCKETS"

"There aren't nearly as many shoe repair shops as there used to be because people don't wear out the soles and heels of shoes by walking on them much anymore."

ANDY ROONEY "THE FOLLOWING THINGS ARE TRUE" FROM
SWEET & SOUR

"Of all exercises walking is the best."

THOMAS JEFFERSON

"You jist make'em walk chalk."

MARK TWAIN
A TRUE STORY

"Peripatetic—The word comes from the Greek and means to walk about. Aristotle and his followers were called peripatetics because they taught or discussed matters while walking or moving about."

HERBERT VICTOR PROCHNOW
THE PUBLIC SPEAKER'S TREASURE CHEST

"Oh, he's a genuine backpacker, all right. He's got a filed-down toothbrush."

OVERHEARD BY COLIN FLETCHER
THE COMPLETE WALKER III

"We've been all the way to the moon and back, but have trouble crossing the street to meet the new neighbor."

ANONYMOUS

"The man who walks takes title to the world around him."

AMERICAN PROVERB

"He knows the way best who went there last."

AMERICAN PROVERB

"I've learned over a period of years there are set-backs when you come up against the immovable object; sometimes the object doesn't move."

COLEMAN YOUNG, CIRCA 1980

"... not a word? ...

They are but burs, cousin, thrown upon thee
in holiday foolery: if we walk not in the trodden
paths our very petticoats will catch them."

WILLIAM SHAKESPEARE
CELIA, *AS YOU LIKE IT,* ACT I, SCENE III

———•••••———

"Although he is no longer the home run king, Babe
Ruth is still the walk king. He received the most
walks in a season, 170 and also for a career, 2,056.
The latter figure means that his walks to first base
alone covered nearly 36 miles."

"THE BASEBALL ENCYCLOPEDIA," 1993 UPDATE, 9TH EDITION,
P. 1421

"Frankly, I fail to see how going for a six-month, thousand-mile walk through deserts and mountains can be judged less real than spending six months working eight hours a day, five days a week, in order to earn enough money to be able to come back to a comfortable home in the evening and sit in front of a TV screen and watch the two-dimensional image of some guy talking about a book he has written on a six-month, thousand-mile walk through deserts and mountains."

COLIN FLETCHER
THE COMPLETE WALKER III

"The civilized man has built a coach, but he has lost the use of his feet."

RALPH WALDO EMERSON

"It is somehow reassuring to discover that the world 'travel' is derived from 'travail,' denoting the pains of childbirth."

JESSICA MITFORD

"We did walk ten paces behind—and the reason was to tell you where to go."

BEA MEDICINE
"ROLES AND FUNCTIONS OF INDIAN WOMEN," IN
INDIAN EDUCATION

"Not at all similar are the race of the immortal gods and the race of men who walk upon the earth."

HOMER
THE ILIAD TRANSLATED BY F. MAX MULLER

"You cannot teach a crab to walk straight."

ARISTOPHANES

———•◦•———

"Where'er you walk, cool gales shall fan the glade, /
Trees, where you sit, shall crowd into a shade: /
Where'er you tread, the blushing flow'rs shall rise, /
And all things flourish where you turn your eyes."

ALEXANDER POPE
"PASTORALS"

———•◦•———

"Why are there trees I never walk under but large
and melodious thoughts descend upon me?"

WALT WHITMAN
"SONG OF THE OPEN ROAD"

"What thoughts I have of you tonight, Walt Whitman, for I walked down the sidestreets under the trees with a headache self-conscious looking at the full moon."

ALLEN GINSBURG,
"A SUPERMARKET IN CALIFORNIA"

"There is a way to walk on water, / And it has something to do with the feel / Of the silken waves sliding continuously / And carefully against the inner arches / Of the feet;"

PATIANN ROGERS
"THERE IS A WAY TO WALK ON WATER"
FIREKEEPER: NEW AND SELECTED POEMS

"However, some of us do walk best under duress. Or only under duress. Certainly my own most memorable hikes can be classified as Shortcuts that Backfired."

EDWARD ABBEY
"WALKING"

―――――・・―――――

"I choose the road from here to there / When I've a scandalous tale to bear, / Tools to return or books to lend / To someone at the other end. //
Returning afterwards, although / I meet my footsteps toe to toe, / The road looks altogether new / Now that is done I meant to do. //
But I avoid it when I take / A walker's walk for walking's sake: / The repetition it involves / Raises a doubt it never solves."

W.H. AUDEN
"WALKS"

"She walks in beauty, like the night of cloudless climes and starry skies; and all that's best of dark and bright meet in her aspect and her eyes."

LORD BYRON

"I think it pisses God off if you walk by the color purple in a field somewhere and don't notice it."

ALICE WALKER
THE COLOR PURPLE

"There's only a short walk from the hallelujah to the hoot."

WILLIAM KENNEDY
ON THE SIMILARITY BETWEEN GOOD WRITING AND POOR WRITING

"The pay is good and I can walk to work."

JOHN F. KENNEDY
ON BECOMING PRESIDENT

———•·•··•———

"Change means movement. Movement means friction. Only in the frictionless vacuum of a nonexistent abstract world can movement or change occur without that abrasive friction of conflict."

SAUL ALINSKY

———•·•··•———

"Golf seems to be an arduous way to go for a walk. I prefer to take the dogs out."

PRINCESS ANNE

"If Abraham Lincoln were elected by the people, President of these United States, I would agree to walk from Boston State House to the Capitol at Washington (a distance of 478 miles) inside of *ten consecutive days*."

EDWARD PAYSON WESTON
FROM HIS 1861 JOURNAL DEPICTING A WAGER WITH
MR. GEORGE B. EDDY OF WORCESTER, MASS.

"All mankind is divided into three classes: those that are immovable, those that are moveable and those that move."

ARABIAN PROVERB

"Isn't it really quite extraordinary to see that, since man took his first step, no one has asked himself why he walks, how he walks, if he has ever walked, if he could walk better, what he achieves in walking . . . questions that are tied to all the philosophical, psychological, and political systems which preoccupy the world."

HONORÉ DE BALZAC
"THÉORIE DE LA DEMARCHÉ"

———

"In my room, the world is beyond my understanding; / But when I walk I see that it consists of three or four hills and a cloud."

WALLACE STEVENS
"OF THE SURFACE OF THINGS"

Obstacles

There are so many reasons not to walk: the shoes pinch, or the road is too long, or maybe you're like Edward Abbey and just think "there's something unnatural about walking." Excuses, excuses! For all the tongue-in-cheek jibes made about walking—most people recognize that there's no real reason not to walk—Orison Swett Marden got it right when he said, "Most of our obstacles would melt away if, instead of cowering before them, we should make up our minds to walk boldly through them."

"Do I suppose this big walk of Mrs. Beach will start all women walking? I hope it will start them to walking to the market or to the grocery store, at least, so that they may pick out their meats and groceries and not have them pitched into the basement door by telephone orders any more. This is the sort of thing that is making the high cost of living."

WILLIAM J. GAYNOR
MAYOR OF NEW YORK CITY IN REPLY TO A REPORTER'S QUERY IN 1912 ABOUT MRS. MINTA BEACH, A 30-SOMETHING WELL-TO-DO NEW YORKER ON HER IMPENDING WALK FROM NEW YORK CITY HALL TO CHICAGO

"You feel so much more positive when you work out. Setbacks are depressing, but you need to forgive yourself for it. If you're not hard on yourself, then you're going to be less hard on other people, and much more optimistic."

TERRY FARRELL,
COSTAR OF CBS-TV'S *BECKER*

"One of the most basic principles of my philosophy of fitness is that everyone can find some time to exercise, even if they have to squeeze it in among their daily chores. So put some spring in that step and let your arms move and pump with you, whether you are enjoying nature's bounty or on a treadmill watching your favorite TV show. You can walk your way to a better body!"

DENISE AUSTIN
HIT THE SPOT!

"Since having my son, I find I have a lot less time to work out, and it's nearly impossible to do it at a scheduled time. I learned to squeeze it in whenever I had a few minutes. . . . My prenatal yoga teacher encouraged us to walk up to five miles a day. I only made it that far once, but I did walk two to three miles a couple times a week. [Now] I do those same walks with my little guy in a sling."

CINDY CRAWFORD

Working out is something I love to do, but with my schedule, it's tough to be consistent. If I'm traveling, I'll walk the airports instead of taking trams. If I'm at home, I either get up before dawn and exercise before my kids are up, or I exercise while I'm spending time with my five girls."

MRS. FIELDS,
THE SURPRISINGLY SLIM WOMAN BEHIND THE COOKIES

"I'm not a fanatic. I listen to my body and take days off. A half-hour walk is only three percent of your time. When you think of it that way, it seems doable."

DENISE AUSTIN
ON WALKING OFF WEIGHT AFTER PREGNANCY

"There's always so much to do that there's a temptation not to exercise. Luckily, my husband is committed to exercise, and we often work out together, which helps. I often exercise while my children are napping in the afternoon. That way, it's an appointment like any other I'm committed to keeping."

HANNAH STORM,
NBC SPORTSCASTER

"When I was pregnant I mostly walked for the exercise. Now I'm adding some weights, yoga, and a little running to my routine. I'm trying to incorporate exercise into my lifestyle."

KELLI WILLIAMS
COSTAR OF ABC'S *THE PRACTICE*

"It seems quite impossible to walk in America."

ROGER BANNISTER

"The Americans *never* walk. In winter too cold and in summer too hot."

J.B. YEATS
LETTERS TO HIS SON, W.B. YEATS AND OTHERS, 1969–1922

"Don't bother about genius. Don't worry about being clever. Trust in hard work, perseverance, and determination. And the best motto for the long march is:"Don't grumble. Plug on!""

FREDERICK TREVES

"The doctor said I had 'walking pneumonia.' 'Why can't I walk, then?' I shot back at him through a fever-induced haze. 'Well,' he said, 'if you want to be technical about it, you have 'lying-around-and-moaning-a-lot pneumonia.'"

DONALD KAUL
COFOUNDER OF RAGBRAI, THE WORLD'S LARGEST BIKE RIDE

"Nearly everyone I talked to has some gruesome story involving a guileless acquaintance who had gone off hiking the trail with high hopes and new boots and come stumbling back two days later with a bobcat attached to his head or dripping blood from an armless sleeve and whispering in a hoarse voice, *'Bear!'* before sinking into a troubled unconsciousness."

BILL BRYSON
A WALK IN THE WOODS

"Top Ten Signs You're an Overweight Cop:
3. Suspect you're pursuing on foot has time to stop at a LensCrafters and get new glasses."

DAVID LETTERMAN,
TOP TEN LIST

"I catch the thin gloom of smog dirtying and blurring the view of the Rocky Mountains and reminding me that—on this Tuesday of business—not all is well and not even a walk can make it so."

JEFFREY C. ROBINSON
THE WALK

"Roads are made for horses and men of business. I do not travel in them much, comparatively, because I am not in a hurry to get to any tavern or grocery or livery-stable or depot to which they lead."

HENRY DAVID THOREAU

"Walking for walking's sake may be highly laudable and exemplary a thing as it is held to be by those who practice it. My objection to it is that it stops the brain."

MAX BEERBOHM
"GOING OUT FOR A WALK"

"I resolved to walk it out of Cheapness; but my unhappy Curiosity is such, that I find it always my Interest to take Coach, for some odd Adventure among Beggars, Ballad Singers, or the like, detains and throws me into Expense."

RICHARD STEELE
TWENTY-FOUR HOURS IN LONDON

"There's man all over for you, blaming on his boots the fault of his feet."

SAMUEL BECKETT
WAITING FOR GODOT, Act 1

"So far as my experience goes, travelers generally exaggerate the difficulties of the way."

HENRY DAVID THOREAU
A WEEK ON THE CONCORD AND MERRIMACK RIVERS: TUESDAY

"To me the outdoors is what you must pass through in order to get from your apartment into a taxicab."

FRAN LEBOWITZ

"My hiking companions went on, but I stopped just where the hillside started down and sat for a while on a lichen-painted wall of gray stone—not so much because I was footsore, but because I felt good and happy, and I wanted to sit on the wall in the Spanish sun and prolong the feeling."

CATHERINE WATSO
"THE SPANISH CHURCH"

—◆◆◆◆—

"Once I decide to do something, I can't have people telling me I can't. If there's a roadblock, you jump over it, walk around it, crawl under it."

KITTY KELLEY

—◆◆◆◆—

"The only reason I would take up jogging is so that I could hear heavy breathing again."

ERMA BOMBECK

"I can remember walking as a child. It was not customary to say you were fatigued. It was customary to complete the goal of the expedition."

KATHARINE HEPBURN

"I was all set to buy one of those Lay-Z-Boy chairs so I could keep my movement to a minimum, when I decided to start walking."

MARJORIE TAYLOR, AGE 68
WALKING MEDICINE BY GARY YANKER AND KATHY BURTON

"But I know that many times when someone has said, 'Come on, let's take a walk . . . visit a friend . . . head for the woods . . . , [sic]' and my sense of duty has cautioned, 'No, you shouldn't, you have to wash your hair . . . scrub the floor . . . clean the oven . . . act your age . . . write the book . . . ,' my disappointment alarm has buzzed and said: '*Those* things you can do tomorrow; but you can't get back today.'"

MAGGIE NICHOLS
WILD, WILD WOMAN

"To: Al Franken . . .

Here then are my suggestions for some simple and easy-to-remember guidelines for the future so that we can continue building on the limited progress we have made so far.

1. *Learn from past mistakes in order to avoid repeating them in the future.* For example: Don't pledge to walk the state as soon as we arrive in a new state."

NORM ORNSTEIN
FRANKEN FOR PRESIDENT

"I will walk on eggs."

THOMAS HEYWOOD
"A WOMAN KILLED WITH KINDNESS"

"Thou sure and firm-set earth, / Hear not my steps, which way they walk, for fear / Thy very stones prate of my whereabout"

WILLIAM SHAKESPEARE
MACBETH, *MACBETH*, Act 2, Scene 1

"I nauseate walking; 'tis a country diversion, I loathe the country."

WILLIAM CONGREVE,
THE WAY OF THE WORLD, Act IV, Scene II

"Most of our obstacles would melt away if, instead of cowering before them, we should make up our minds to walk boldly through them."

ORISON SWETT MARDEN

"Life's up and downs provide windows of opportunity to determine your values and goals. Think of using all obstacles as stepping stones to build the life you want."

MARSHA SINETAR

⊶•⊷

"Oh! no indeed! walking up that hill again would do her more harm than any sitting down could do her good;"

JANE AUSTEN
PERSUASION

"A walk? Why should he take Foster for a walk, show him his beloved country, point out those curves and lines and hollows the long silver shield of Ullswater, the cloudy purple hills hunched like blankets about the knees of some recumbent giant? Why? It was as though he had turned round to someone behind him and had said, 'You have some further design in this.'"

HUGH WALPOLE
"THE TARN"

"There is something unnatural about walking. Especially walking uphill, which always seems to me not only unnatural but so *unnecessary*. That iron tug of gravitation should be all the reminder we need that in walking uphill we are violating a basic law of nature. Yet we persist in doing it. No one can explain why. George H. Leigh-Mallory's asinine rationale for climbing a mountain—'because it's there'— could easily be refuted with a few well-placed hydrogen bombs. But our common sense continues to lag far behind the available technology."

EDWARD ABBEY
"WALKING"

"The Table and the Chair

I

Said the Table to the Chair,
'You can hardly be aware,
'How I suffer from the heat,
'And from the chilblains on my feet!
'If we took a little walk,
'We might have a little talk!
'Pray let us take the air!'
Said the Table to the Chair.

II
Said the Chair to the Table,
'Now you know we are not able!
'How foolishly you talk,
'When you know we cannot walk!'
Said the Table with a sigh,
'It can do no harm to try,
'I've as many legs as you,
'Why can't we walk on two?'"

EDWARD LEAR,
THE TABLE AND THE CHAIR

"Unite to move forward."

HAWAIIAN PROVERB

"What you know is merely a point of departure. So let's move."

KEORAPETSE KGOSITSILE

———

"Plenty sits still, hunger is a wanderer."

SOUTH AFRICAN PROVERB

———

"Motivation is what gets you started. Habit is what keeps you going."

JIM RYUN
WOMAN'S WORLD

"Top Ten Signs You're Not Going to Win the New York City Marathon:
3. You get winded licking stamps."

DAVID LETTERMAN,
TOP TEN LIST

Pace

A slow pace is the one usually associated with walking. But the competitive walkers of the nineteenth century and modern fitness walkers alike would disagree. So would Charles Dickens: "If I could not walk far and fast, I think I should just explode and perish." Nevertheless, many of us still celebrate the ways in which walking slows us down. Walking often feels like the pace intended by nature and the only speed at which one can truly appreciate the world. Wendell Berry says, "Our senses, after all, were developed to function at foot speeds." Others invoke the association of slowness with deliberation and persistence, that ultimately leads to success. Remember Aesop's Tortoise and the Hare?

"Adopt the pace of nature: her secret is patience."

RALPH WALDO EMERSON

"To enjoy city walking to the utmost you have to throw yourself into a mood of loving humanity."

DONALD CULROSS PEATTIE
NEW YORK TIMES MAGAZINE, April 5, 1942

"Never walk fast in the streets, which is a mark of vulgarity . . . though it may be tolerable in a tradesman."

LORD CHESTERFIELD
LETTERS

"I am a slow walker, but I never walk backwards."

ABRAHAM LINCOLN

"Once off the freeway, my pace gradually slowed, as the roads became progressively more primitive, from seventy miles an hour to a walk. And now, here at my camping place, I have stopped altogether. But my mind is still keyed to seventy miles an hour . . . Having come here by the freeway, my mind is not so fully here as it would have been if I had come by the crookeder, slower state roads; it is incalculably father away than it would have been if I had come all the way on foot, as my earlier predecessors came . . . Our senses, after all, were developed to function at foot speeds."

WENDELL BERRY
"AN ENTRANCE TO THE WOODS"

"If I could not walk far and fast, I think I should just explode and perish."

CHARLES DICKENS

"Runners may think fastwalking is lame, but step for step, the waddlers may be getting a better workout."

JOANNE CHEN
"WALK THIS WAY," FROM *WOMEN'S SPORTS AND FITNESS*,
SEPTEMBER 1999

"The distinction between running and walking is very complicated. A man gets three warnings and then is waved off. If the knee of his front leg isn't locked when the leg touches the ground, if he doesn't place his forward heel on the ground before his rear toe leaves the ground, or if both feet are up in the air at the same time, then he's *running*."

HARRY RAPPAPORT, ON THE RULES OF RACEWALKING
THE NEW YORKER, JUNE 19, 1948

"One day, on my asking him why he took such long steps in walking, a Scottish friend of mine replied: 'Whin I was a wee lad me mither used to say to me, "'Laddie, whin ye're a walkin' ye should take longer steps an' wear yer brogs the less the mile.'"

HERBERT VICTOR PROCHOW
THE PUBLIC SPEAKER'S TREASURE CHEST

"Limping along paths of crushed stone and tapping his cane as he took each step, he raced across intricacies of sunlight and shadow spread before him on the dark garden floor like golden lace."

MARK HELPRIN
A SOLDIER OF THE GREAT WAR

"When I was a child, I loved the last movement of Beethoven's *Ninth Symphony*, as does everybody. I loved the chorus singing the 'Ode to Joy . . .'

But in these last few years . . . it was the Second Movement that really belonged to me.

It's like walking music, the music of someone walking doggedly and almost vengefully up a mountain. It just goes on and on and on, as though the person won't stop walking. Then it comes to a quiet place, as if in the Vienna Woods, as if the person is suddenly breathless and exultant and has the view of the city that he wants, and can throw up his arms, and dance in a circle.

. . . then the drums come. And the uphill walk begins again, the determined walking and walking. Walking and walking . . . "

ANNE RICE
VIOLIN

"Mr. Sanderson leaned forward.'How do they *feel*?'

The boy looked down at his feet deep in the rivers, in the fields of wheat, in the wind that already was rushing him out of the town. He looked up at the old man, his eyes burning, his mouth moving, but no sound came out.

'Antelopes?' said the old man, looking from the boy's face to his shoes.'Gazelles?'

The boy thought about it, hesitated, and nodded a quick nod. Almost immediately he vanished. He just spun about with a whisper and went off. The door stood empty. The sound of the tennis shoes faded in the jungle heat."

RAY BRADBURY
DANDELION WINE

"I'm sure nobody walks much faster than I do."

LEWIS CARROLL

"'A pedestrian calling himself Prof. E.S. Hidden is credited with walking forty miles in seven hours, forty-three minutes and thirty seconds,' *The Sportsman* said, sneeringly, in 1878. 'It's slow enough to be true.'"

WALTER BERNSTEIN and MILTON MELTZER
"A WALKING FEVER," *VIRGINIA QUARTERLY REVIEW*

"We must walk before we run."

GEORGE BORROW

"He that goes softly, goes safely."

WILLIAM ROBERTSON
PHRASEOLOGIA GENERALIS (1681)

"The swiftest traveler is he that goes afoot."

HENRY DAVID THOREAU
"ECONOMY," FROM *WALDEN*

"When you stroll you never hurry back, because if you had anything to do, you wouldn't be strolling in the first place."

VIRGINIA CARY HUDSON
O YE JIGS AND JULEPS

"On an unknown path every foot is slow."

AMERICAN PROVERB

"Hare: This is a silly, silly race. I'm so far ahead I can't even see poor Mr. Tortoise. I think I'll take a little nap in this cool grass."

AESOP'S FABLES

"'Being quick on your feet is a fine thing, but slow and steady wins the race,' said Mr. Tortoise."

AESOP'S FABLES

"An ant on the move does more than a dozing ox."

MEXICAN PROVERB

"Life is so short we must move very slowly."

THAI PROVERB

"Wherefore are these things hid? Wherefore have these gifts a curtain before'em?...
My very walk should be a jig; I would not so much as make water but in a sink-a-pace."

WILLIAM SHAKESPEARE
SIR TOBY BELCH, *TWELFTH NIGHT*, ACT I, SCENE III

"Mostly, two miles an hour is good going."

COLIN FLETCHER
THE COMPLETE WALKER III

"There is more to life than increasing its speed."

GANDHI

"One can never consent to creep when one feels an impulse to soar."

HELEN KELLER

"Life set itself to new processions of seed-time and harvest, the skin newly turned to seasonal variations, the very blood humming to new altitudes. The rhythm of walking, always a recognizable background for our thoughts, altered from the militaristic stride to the jog of the wide unrutted earth."

MARY HUNTER AUSTIN
THE AMERICAN RHYTHM

"Feet that run on willing errands!"

LONGFELLOW
"HIAWATHA," PT/ X, L. 33

"a long walk
a long
walk a long
walk a long
walk along"

ROBERT GRENIER
"A LONG WALK"

"'Will you walk a little faster?' said a whiting to a snail, / 'There's a porpoise close behind us, and he's treading on my tail.'"

LEWIS CARROL
ALICE'S ADVENTURES IN WONDERLAND

"When he ran from a cop his transitions from accelerating walk to easy jog trot to brisk canter to headlong gallop to flogged-piston sprint . . . were as distinct and as soberly in order as an automatic gearshift."

JAMES AGEE
SPEAKING OF COMEDIAN BUSTER KEATON
"COMEDY'S GREATEST ERA" REPRINTED IN *LIFE*, FALL 1986

"The lame man who keeps the right road outstrips the runner who keeps the wrong one."

AMERICAN PROVERB

"Alessandro Guiliani believed that if all things went smoothly and well on a journey, the momentum and equanimity of walking or riding would over-shadow whatever the traveler had left behind and whatever he was traveling to reach. Making good time on the road was in itself reason for elation."

MARK HELPRIN
A SOLDIER OF THE GREAT WAR

"Some people walk with both eyes focused on their goal: the highest mountain peak in the range, the fifty-mile marker, the finish line. They stay motivated by anticipating the end of the journey. Since I tend to be easily distracted, I travel somewhat differently—one step at a time, with many pauses in between."

HANNAH NYALA
POINT LAST SEEN

The Path

A path can be physical and specific, or conceptual. It can be a route through the wilderness or a road to success. Those who look for paths discover there are many ways to approach them, to identify them, and to imagine or realize their destinations. Some speak of being daunted by the length or difficulty of the path, others of moving forward, still others of the best way to help companions along. And finally, Ralph Waldo Emerson counsels, "Do not go where the path may lead; go instead where there is no path and leave a trail."

"As we roamed the heights of the Presidential Range, John and I shared the feelings of the tramper who said:'I consider a hiker with a pack on his back as a self-sufficient individual, with all the petty entanglements of his life brushed aside like cobwebs."

ANDREW H. BROWN
"SKYLINE TRAIL FROM MAINE TO GEORGIA," FROM
NATIONAL GEOGRAPHIC

"It is good to have an end to journey towards; but it is the journey that matters in the end."

URSULA K. LEGUIN
"THE LEFT HAND OF DARKNESS"

"The clearest way to the Universe is through a forest wilderness."

JOHN MUIR

"All paths lead to nowhere, so it is important to choose a path that has heart."

CARLOS CASTAÑEDA
THE TEACHINGS OF DON JUAN

"I don't really have studios. I wander around, around people, attics, out in fields, in cellars, anyplace I find that invites me."

ANDREW WYETH
TIME, AUGUST 18, 1986

". . . focus on the journey, not the destination. Joy is found not in finishing an activity but in doing it."

GREG ANDERSON

"Accomplishments will prove to be a journey, not a destination."

DWIGHT D. EISENHOWER
SPEECH DECEMBER 16, 1957

"If we are always arriving and departing, it is also true that we are eternally anchored. One's destination is never a place but rather a new way of looking at things."

HENRY MILLER

"And a highway shall be there, and a way, and in it shall be called the way of holiness; the unclean shall not pass over it; but it shall be for those: the wayfaring men, through fools shall not err therein."

ISAIAH 35:8

"Common sense and nature will do a lot to make the pilgrimage of life not too difficult."

W. SOMERSET MAUGHAM

"Do not go where the path may lead; go instead where there is no path and leave a trail."

RALPH WALDO EMERSON
"JOURNEY IN WORD"

"I who had only wanted a quiet walk, have become the owl and the fox. I, who had gone only to listen, have become the one was listened to."

GENE HILL
"A LISTENING WALK" FROM *FIELD & STREAM*

"Who could say the words 'Great Smoky Mountains' or 'Shenandoah Valley' and not feel an urge, as the naturalist John Muir once put it, to 'throw a loaf of bread and a pound of tea in an old sack and jump over the back fence'?"

BILL BRYSON
A WALK IN THE WOODS

———•+•+•———

"I am very, very blessed. The Valley is full of people, but they do not annoy me. I revolve in pathless places and in higher rocks than *the world* and his ribbony wife can reach."

JOHN MUIR
TO YOSEMITE AND BEYOND

"'Would you tell me, please, which way I ought to go from here?'

'That depends a good deal on where you want to go to,' said the Cat.

'I don't much care where . . . ' said Alice.

'Then it doesn't matter which way you go,' said the Cat.

'. . . so long as I get *somewhere*,' Alice added as an explanation.

'Oh, you're sure to do that,' said the Cat, 'if you only walk long enough.'"

LEWIS CARROLL
ALICE IN WONDERLAND

"Two roads diverged in a wood, and I—
I took the one less traveled by,
And that has made all the difference."

ROBERT FROST
"TWO ROADS"

"'If this road goes in, it must come out,' said the
Scarecrow, 'and as the Emerald City is at the other
end of the road, we must go wherever it leads us.'"

L. FRANK BAUM
THE NEW WIZARD OF OZ

"I was very young when I first saw the road that matched my desire, a bright highway that wound between sloping hills more beautiful than any the poets have sung."

SEOSAMH MAC GRIANNA
"MY OWN ROAD"

———

"He's like to fall who runs on the wall.
He's safe and sound on level ground."

FERNAN DE ROJAS
CELESTINA, *LA CELESTINA*, ACT XI,

———

"May you have the hindsight to know where you have been, and the foresight to know where you're going, and the insight to know when you're going too far."

IRISH TOAST

"Travel reaches toleration."

BENJAMIN DISRAELI

"The sure traveler,
Though he alight sometimes, still goeth on."

GEORGE HERBERT
"THE CHURCH-PORCH"

"For always roaming with a hungry heart,
Much have I seen and known."

ALFRED, LORD TENNYSON
"ULYSSES"

"Not to go back is somewhat to advance, / And men must walk, at least, before they dance."

> ALEXANDER POPE
> "IMITATIONS OF HORACE, EPILOGUE TO THE SATIRES"

"He wisely walketh that doth safely go."

> BODENHAM

"From the lowest depth there is a path to the loftiest height."

> THOMAS CARLYLE
> SARTOR RESARTUS, Book III

"So I say, 'every path has its puddle,' and try to play gayly with the tadpoles in my puddle."

LOUISA MAY ALCOTT,
LETTER TO HER SISTER

"The longest road is sometimes the shortest way home."

FRANK ROONEY

"Let him that would move the world, first move himself."

SOCRATES

"Where there's a will there's a way."

PROVERB

"A fool and water will go the way they are diverted".

ETHIOPIAN PROVERB

"It is a long lane that has no turning."

PROVERB

"The beaten path is the safest."

LATIN PROVERB

"Towering genius disdains a beaten path."

ABRAHAM LINCOLN

1."In the name of Allah, Most Gracious, Most Merciful.
6. Show us the straight way."

QUAR'AN, FROM AL-FATIHA, OR, THE OPENING CHAPTER

"There are two mistakes one can make along the road to truth—not going all the way, and not starting."

BUDDHA

"Success is a journey not a destination. The doing is usually more important than the outcome. Not everyone can be Number 1."

ARTHUR ASHE

"No life is so hard that you can't make it easier by the way you take it."

ELLEN GLASGOW

"On the human chessboard, all moves are possible."

MIRIAM SCHIFF

"Sooner or later we all discover that the important moments in life are not the advertised ones, not the birthdays, the graduations, the weddings, not the great goals achieved. The real milestones are less prepossessing. They come to the door of memory."

SUSAN B. ANTHONY

"When you come to the fork in the road, take it."

YOGI BERRA
THE YOGI BOOK

"Better to ask twice than to lose your way once."

DANISH PROVERB

"I dreamed a thousand new paths. I woke and walked my old one."

CHINESE PROVERB

"To learn something new, take the path that you took yesterday."

JOHN BURROUGHS

"Instead walk alone in the evening/ heading out of town toward the fields / asleep under a darkening sky; / the dust risen from your steps transforms/ itself into a golden rain fallen / earthward as a gift from no known god."

PHILIP LEVINE
"ASK FOR NOTHING" FROM *THE SIMPLE TRUTH*

"I walked through the wilderness of this world."

JOHN BUNYAN
PILGRIM'S PROGRESS, Part I

"The beaten path grows no grass."

JEAN DE CONDE
RECEUIL DES FABLIAUX

"These people go out into the street, and walk down the street alone. They keep walking, and walk straight out of the city of Omelas, through the beautiful gates. They keep walking across the farmlands of Omelas. Each one goes alone, youth or girl, man or woman. Night falls; the traveler must pass down village streets, between the houses with yellow-lit windows, and on into the darkness of the fields. Each alone, they go west or north, toward the mountains. They go on. They leave Omelas, they walk ahead into the darkness, and they do not come back . . . they seem to know where they are going, the ones who walk away from Omelas."

URSULA K. LEGUIN
"THE ONES WHO WALK AWAY FROM OMELAS"

"To know the universe itself as a road, as many roads, as roads for traveling souls."

WALT WHITMAN
"SONG OF THE OPEN ROAD"

"Beaten paths are for beaten men."

ERIC A. JOHNSTON

"Genius and stupidity never stray from their respective paths; talent wanders to and fro, following every light."

GEORGE MOORE

"The obstacle is the path."

ZEN PROVERB

"Stride forward with a firm, steady step knowing with a deep, certain inner knowing that you will reach every goal you set yourselves, that you will achieve every aim."

EILEEN CADDY

—•—

"So you are lean and mean and resourceful and you continue to walk on the edge of the precipice because over the years you have become fascinated by how close you can walk without losing your balance."

RICHARD M. NIXON

—•—

"One who keeps on his toes is never down at the heels."

PROVERB

"It's not so much where you are as which way you are going."

AMERICAN PROVERB

"Every path hath a puddle."

GEORGE HERBERT
"JACULA PRUDENTUM"

"Walk away from it until you're stronger. All your problems will be there when you get back, but you'll be better able to cope."

LADY BIRD JOHNSON

"Life's but a walking shadow, a poor player
That struts and frets his hour upon the stage
And then is heard no more: it is a tale
Told by an idiot, full of sound and fury,
Signifying nothing."

WILLIAM SHAKESPEARE
MACBETH, *MACBETH* ACT V, SCENE V

"Happiness is not a station you arrive at, but a manner of traveling."

MARGARET LEE RUNBECK

"Life is just a short walk from the cradle to the grave—and it sure behooves us to be kind to one another along the way."

ALICE CHILDRESS

"Every life is a march from innocence, through temptation, to virtue or vice."

LYMAN ABBOTT

———•✦•———

"May the lilt of Irish laughter
Lighten every load,
May the mist of Irish magic
Shorten every road,
May you taste the sweetest pleasures
That fortune ere bestowed,
And may all your friends remember
All the favors you are owed."

IRISH BLESSING

"I am too old . . . I remain the primitive of the path I opened up."

PAUL CÉZANNE

"Any intelligent fool can make things bigger, more complex, and more violent. It takes a touch of genius—and a lot of courage—to move in the opposite direction."

ERNST FRITZ SCHUMACHER

"Paths can't be made without feet."

ANN RADCLIFFE
THE ROMANCE OF THE FOREST

Spirituality

If walking is the most natural human connection to the earth, it's also a bridge to whatever exists beyond. God, spirituality, and walking are often connected. Spiritual people are said to walk with God, a metaphor used repeatedly to describe the possibility of a personal relationship with God. "The Prayer of the Tired Walker" ("If you pick 'em up, O Lord, I'll put 'em down") and the Book of Micah ("What doth the Lord require of thee, but to do justly, and to love mercy, and to walk humbly with thy God?") offer varying glimpses into that personal relationship. Walking also engenders a kind of religious experience not necessarily associated with any particular sect. Internal peace and self-discovery are effects that can be attributed to the act itself or to the great unseen forces of nature. In either case, walking puts us in touch with worlds of which we may only have the vaguest sense.

"I like to walk about amidst the beautiful things that adorn the world; but private wealth I should decline, or any sort of personal possession, because they would take away my liberty."

GEORGE SANTAYANA

"If you can walk with crowds and keep your virtue, Or walk with Kings—nor lose the common torch . . . Yours is the Earth and everything that's in it, And—which is more—you'll be a Man, my son!"

RUDYARD KIPLING

"No matter how far a person can go, the horizon is still way beyond you."

ZORA NEAL HURSTON

"Your feet will bring you where your heart is."

IRISH PROVERB

"Men go abroad to admire the heights of the mountains . . . and yet pass themselves by."

ST. AUGUSTINE
CONFESSIONS

"A sedentary life is the real sin against the Holy Spirit. Only those thoughts that come by walking have any value."

NIETZSCHE
"MAXIMS AND MISSILES," 34

"all ignorance toboggans into know / and trudges up to ignorance again"

E. E. CUMMINGS
"ONE TIMES ONE"

———•••••———

"Man, unlike any other thing organic or inorganic in the universe, grows beyond his work, walks up the stairs of his concepts, emerges ahead of his accomplishments."

JOHN STEINBECK
THE GRAPES OF WRATH

———•••••———

"What do suppose will satisfy the soul, except to walk free and own no superior?"

WALT WHITMAN
LEAVES OF GRASS

"Have I not walked without an upward look / Of caution under stars that very well / Might not have missed me when they shot and fell? / It was a risk I had to take—and took."

ROBERT FROST
"BRAVADO"

"Great Spirit, help me never to judge another until I have walked in his moccasins."

SIOUX INDIAN PRAYER

"Oh! for a closer walk with God,
A calm and heav'nly frame;
A light to shine upon the road
That leads me to the Lamb!"

WILLIAM COWPER

"There's a long, long trail a-winding into the land of my dreams."

> STODDARD KING, JR.,
> "THE LONG, LONG TRAIL"

"I believe that there is a subtle magnetism in Nature, which, if we unconsciously yield to it, will direct us aright."

> HENRY DAVID THOREAU
> "WALKING"

"they shall walk with joy in a green meadow"
"enter Paradise, you and your wives, walking with joy"

> QUAR'AN
> A CONCORDANCE OF THE QUAR'AN, 30:15 & 43:70.

"What doth the Lord require of thee, but to do justly, and to love mercy, and to walk humbly with thy God?"

MICAH 6:8

"You got to walk that lonesome valley, you got to walk it for yourself. Nobody here can walk it for you, you got to walk it for yourself."

SPIRITUAL

"We were on our way to the great shrine of Saint James in the city of Santiago de Compostela, which made all of us pilgrims of some sort. But none of us were religious ones; blisters and stiff muscles aside, we saw no merit in suffering."

CATHERINE WATSON
"THE SPANISH CHURCH"

"If you pick'em up, O Lord, I'll put'em down."

THE PRAYER OF THE TIRED WALKER

———

"If the sight of the blue skies fills you with joy, if a blade of grass springing up in the fields has power to move you, if the simple things of nature have a message that you understand, rejoice, for your soul is alive."

ELEONORA DUSE
ACTORS ON ACTING, PART II

———

"Heaven is under our feet as well as over our heads."

HENRY DAVID THOREAU
"THE POND IN WINTER," FROM *WALDEN*

"King Christ, this world is all aleak; / and life pre-servers there are none: / and waves which only He may walk / Who dares to call Himself a man.

E. E. CUMMINGS
"JEHOVAH BURIED, SATAN DEAD"

"Stand ye in the ways, and see, and ask for the old paths, where is the good way, and walk therein."

JEREMIAH 6:16

"We walk by faith, not by sight."

CORINTHIANS 5:7

"Darest thou now O soul, / Walk out with me toward the unknown region / Where neither ground is for the feet nor any path to follow?"

WALT WHITMAN
LEAVES OF GRASS

"Let us walk honestly, as in the day."

ROMANS 13:13

"Millions of spiritual creatures walk the earth/ Unseen, both when we wake, and when we sleep."

JOHN MILTON
PARADISE LOST

"Walk while ye have the light, lest darkness come upon you."

JOHN 12:35

"Hear the voice of the Bard! / Who Present, Past, and Future, sees; / Whose ears have heard / The Holy Word / That walk'd among the ancient trees."

WILLIAM BLAKE
"SONGS OF EXPERIENCE"

"Of him who walked in glory and joy."

WILLIAM WORDSWORTH
"RESOLUTION"

"Blessed is the man that walketh not in the counsel of the ungodly."

PSALM 1:1

———

"Who layeth the beams of his chambers in the waters: who maketh the clouds his chariot: who walketh upon the wings of the wind."

PSALM 104:3

"Jesus went unto them, walking on the sea."

MATTHEW 14:25

———

"As long as the road is, even if it ends in dust, the gods come with us, keeping a watchful eye."

MATSUO BASHO
"THE NARROW ROAD TO THE INTERIOR"

"Gently did my soul / Put off her veil, and, self-transmuted, stood / Naked as in the presence of her God. / As on I walked, a comfort seem'd to touch / A heart that had not been disconsolate, / Strength came where weakness was not known to be, / At least not felt; and restoration came, / Like an intruder, knocking at the door / Of unacknowledg'd weariness."

WILLIAM WORDSWORTH
"THE PRELUDE" (1805)

"He who leaveth home in search of knowledge walketh in the path of God."

MOHAMMED

"The solitary, pensive walker draws a singular drunkenness from this universal communion. He who can easily blend into the crowd knows feverish pleasures, which will be eternally denied to the egoist, closed like a strong-box, and the sluggard, shut up like a mollusk. He adopts as his own all the professions, all the joys, and all the miseries that circumstances present to him."

CHARLES BAUDELAIRE
"CROWDS"

Style

Sometimes walking is all about style. It's amazing that the one word can encompass both Marilyn Monroe's sashay and the crumpling progress of the Scarecrow in the Wizard of Oz. There truly is an "art of walking," as Dr. M. Beckett Howorth claims. "To walk" is never just to walk; what you really do is stride, amble, saunter, limp, shuffle, strut, or mince. The style you use might be the result of your gender, the type of shoe you're wearing, the era in which you live, or the reason for which you're walking.

"You know as much of the art of walking as I do."

Dr. M. Beckett Howorth
Consumer Bulletin (1973)

"A gentleman, whether walking with two ladies or one, takes the curb side of the pavement. He should never sandwich himself between them.

A young man walking with a young woman should be careful that his manner in no way draws attention to her or to himself.

And it is scarcely necessary to add that no gentleman walks along the street chewing gum or, if he is walking with a lady, puffing a cigar or a cigarette."

Emily Post

"As for the Scarecrow, having no brains, he walked straight ahead, and so stepped into the holes and fell at full length on the hard bricks."

> L. FRANK BAUM
> *THE NEW WIZARD OF OZ*

"Boots and shoes are the greatest trouble of my life. Everything else one can turn and turn about, and make old look like new; but there's no coaxing boots and shoes to look better than they are."

> GEORGE ELIOT

"Wounded vanity knows when it is mortally hurt; and limps off the field, piteous, all disguises thrown away. But pride carries its banner to the last; and fast as it is driven from one field unfurls it in another."

> HELEN HUNT JACKSON
> *RAMONA* (1884)

"Oh, she walked unaware of her own increasing beauty / That was holding men's thoughts from market or plough."

PATRICK MACDONAGH
"SHE WALKED UNAWARE"

"The outlook was frightening; but it was better to walk in your bare feet. It was better to walk without shoes and barefooted than to walk without dignity."

JAMES (KELLY) PLUNKET
"WEEP FOR OUR PRIDE"

"What are you interested in becoming?
'A movie star like Marilyn Monroe.'
Why?
'I like the way she walks.'"

ART LINKLETTER
THE NEW KIDS SAY THE DARNDEST THINGS

"I's a-gwyne to make you walk as straight as a string."

MARK TWAIN
PUDD'NHEAD WILSON

"He went back through the Wet Wild Woods, waving his wild tail, and walking by his wild lone. But he never told anybody."

RUDYARD KIPLING
THE CAT THAT WALKED HIMSELF

"Daisy is walking a drum tune. You can almost hear it by looking at the way she walks."

ZORA NEALE HURSTON
THEIR EYES WERE WATCHING GOD

"Keep the juices flowing by jangling around gently as you move."

SATCHEL PAIGE

"I grant I never saw a goddess go; / My mistress, when she walks, treads on the ground."

SHAKESPEARE
SONNETS NO. CXXX

"'Tis he, I ken the manner of his gait;
He rises on the toe: that spirit of his
In aspiration lifts him from earth."

SHAKESPEARE
ULYSSES, *TROILUS AND CRESSIDA*, ACT IV, SCENE V

"Anyone old enough to read has almost certainly grown too set in the way he puts one foot in front of the other to alter it materially without devoting a great deal of time and determination to the task."

COLIN FLETCHER
THE COMPLETE WALKER III

"Contrary to popular cable TV-induced opinion, aerobics have absolutely nothing to do with squeezing your body into hideous shiny Spandex, grinning like a deranged orangutan, and doing cretinous dance steps to debauched disco music."

CYNTHIA HEIMEL

"She walked with a proud, defiant step, like a martyr to the Coliseum."

HONORE DE BALZAC
COUSIN BETTE

———•◦•◦•———

"If our feet are now so severed from the natural ground, they have inevitably lost life and strength by the separation. It is only the entirely unshod that have lively feet. Watch a peasant who never wears shoes, except for a few unkind hours once a week, and you may see the play of his talk in his mobile feet; they become as dramatic as his hands."

ALICE MEYNELL
"THE FOOT"

"Lord, what would they say/ Did their Catullus walk that way?"

WILLIAM BUTLER YEATS
"THE SCHOLARS"

"Though the Philistines may jostle, you will rank as an apostle in the high aesthetic band, / If you walk down Piccadilly with a poppy or a lily in your medieval hand. / And everyone will say, / As you walk your flowery way, / 'If he's content with a vegetable love, which would certainly not suit *me*, / Why, what a most particularly pure young man this pure young man must be!'"

WILLIAM SCHWENCK GILBERT
"PATIENCE"

"We shall walk in velvet shoes: / Wherever we go / Silence will fall like dews / On white silence below."

ELINOR HOYT WHITE
"VELVET SHOES"

"Her walk revealed her as a true goddess."

VIRGIL
AENEID

"Only a man harrowing clods / In a slow silent walk / With an old horse that stumbles and nods / Half asleep as they stalk."

THOMAS HARDY
"IN TIME OF 'THE BREAKING OF NATIONS'"

"I shall wear white flannel trousers, and walk upon the beach."

T. S. ELIOT,
THE LOVE SONG OF J. ALFRED PRUFROCK

"[The women of Zion] walk with stretched forth necks and wanton eyes, walking and mincing as they go."

ISAIAH 3:16

"He glittered when he walked."

EDWIN ARLINGTON ROBINSON
RICHARD CORY

"Speak in French when you can't think of the English for a thing—turn out your toes when you walk—and remember who you are!"

LEWIS CARROLL
THROUGH THE LOOKING GLASS

"For there's more enterprise / In walking naked"

WILLIAM BUTLER YEATS
"A COAT"

"First the willowy man in the blue cloak; / he didn't say a thing. He counted his toes. / His step ate up the road, / a yard at a time, without bruising a thistle."

RAINER MARIA RILKE
"ORPHEUS, EURYDICE, AND HERMES," TRANSLATED BY
ROBERT LOWELL IN *IMITATIONS*

"The very way that Foster walked bespoke the man. He was always a little ahead of you, pushing his long, thin body along with little eager jerks as though did he not hurry he would miss something that would be immensely to his advantage."

HUGH WALPOLE
"THE TARN," TRANSLATED BY ROBERT LOWELL

"'Tis she who nightly strowls with saunt'ring pace"

JOHN GAY
"TRIVIA; OR, THE ART OF WALKING THE STREETS OF LONDON," TRANSLATED BY ROBERT LOWELL

"But I know that it is possible to live even with worn-out shoes. During the German occupation I was alone here in Rome, and I only had one pair of shoes. If I had taken them to the cobbler's I would have had to stay in bed for two or three days, and in my situation that was impossible. So I continued to wear them and when-on top of everything else-it rained, I felt them gradually falling apart, becoming soft and shapeless, and I felt the coldness of the pavement beneath the soles of my feet."

Natalia Ginzburg
"Worn-Out Shoes,"translated by Robert Lowell

"[He] intuitively choreographed his motions with a body language that projected the image of an eager, bouncy terrier. His walk was jaunty and his manner defiant."

PETER B. FLINT on JAMES CAGNEY
NEW YORK TIMES MARCH 31, 1986

"They all had that sort of dutiful, forward-tilted gait that East Side dowagers get after twenty years of walking small dogs up and down Park Avenue."

TOM WOLFE
ON WOMEN MEETING FOR LUNCH
NEW YORK HERALD TRIBUNE DECEMBER 8, 1963

"My shoes are special . . . shoes for discerning feet."

MANOLO BLAHNIK
ON SHOES FOR WINTER
W MAGAZINE (1986)

———•◦•◦•———

"A woman is known by her walking and drinking."

PROVERB

Time and Place

Sometimes the joy of walking comes from walking in a particular place during a particular season or at a particular time of day. "Place" might be anything from a special room to a certain city to a type of terrain—any location that evokes a specific feeling unique to the environment. From the streets and lanes of Europe, to the Appalachian Trail, to a highway described in Isaiah, it becomes clear that it isn't just the fact that one walks, but where one walks that matters.

"Life for two weeks on the mountain top would show many things about life during the other fifty weeks down below."

BENTON MACKAYE,
FOUNDER OF THE APPALACHIAN TRAIL

———•••••———

"I still love to go back to Mitchell and wander up and down those streets. It just kind of reassures me again that there is a place that I know thoroughly, where the roots are deep. Everything had a place, a specific definition."

GEORGE MCGOVERN
ON HIS HOMETOWN

"The Sussex lanes were lovely in autumn . . . spend-thrift gold and glory of the year-end . . . earth scents and the sky winds and all the magic of the country-side which is ordained for the healing of the soul.

MONICA BALDWIN
"I LEAP OVER THE WALL"

"I had started out with a sense of bitterness about what my country appeared to be. But with every step I had learned otherwise. I had been turned on by America and its people in a thousand fantastic ways."

PETER JENKINS
A WALK ACROSS AMERICA

"Mountains are earth's undying monuments."

NATHANIEL HAWTHORNE

"When a traveler asked Wordsworth's servant to show him her master's study, she answered, 'Here is his library, but his study is out of doors.'"

HENRY DAVID THOREAU
"WALKING"

"As the foxhunter hunts in order to preserve the breed of foxes, and the golfer plays in order that open spaces may be preserved from the builders, so when the desire comes upon us to go street rambling a pencil does for a pretext, and getting up we say: 'Really I must buy a pencil,' as if under cover of this excuse we could indulge safely in the greatest pleasure of town life in winter—rambling the streets of London."

VIRGINIA WOOLF
"STREET HAUNTING"

"The Promised Land always lies on the other side of a wilderness."

HAVELOCK ELLIS

———

"... every road in Ulster veined my heart."

ROY MCFADDEN
"CUCHULAINN"

———

"Won't you come into the garden?
I would like my roses to see you."

SPOKEN TO A YOUNG LADY, AND ATTRIBUTED TO
RICHARD BRINSLEY SHERIDAN

"Another 1956 development that would have a major impact on the American way of life was the completion of the first enclosed shopping mall. It's difficult to imagine now, but back in the pre-mall era, shoppers had to physically go outdoors to get from one store to another, and there were some communities that—prepare to be stunned—*did not have a Gap...*"

DAVE BARRY
DAVE BARRY TURNS 50

"You don't know what a country we have got till you start prowling around it. Personally, I like the small places and sparsely populated states."

WIL ROGERS

"At Bunsen Motors, the sidewalk begins. . . . It is a quiet town, where much of the day you could stand in the middle of Main Street and not be in anyone's way—not forever, but for as long as a person would want to stand in the middle of a street."

GARRISON KEILLOR
LAKE WOBEGONE DAYS

———————

"Under a blazing mid-afternoon summer sky, we see the Seine flooded with sunshine . . . people are strolling, others are sitting or stretched out lazily on the bluish grass."

GEORGES SEURAT

"I walked barefoot—the only way to walk on a muddy road. The earth is softer in Taveuni than in other places, and darker. It's how the earth must have been millions of years ago, in the world's warm beginnings."

LAURIE GOUGH
"LIGHT ON A MOONLESS NIGHT"

"I know I am lucky, of course. I now live in shruburbia . . . But even in cities—most cities, anyway—there are parks; and you can often walk along riverbanks or seashore or across pieces of 'wasteland'—our term for urban land not yet consumed by Mammon."

COLIN FLETCHER
THE SECRET WORLDS OF COLIN FLETCHER

"It was cold and windy, scarcely the day / to take a walk on that long beach. / Everything was withdrawn as far as possible, / indrawn: the tide far out, the ocean shrunken, / seabirds in ones or twos. / The rackety, icy, offshore wind / numbed our faces on one side; / disrupted the formation / of a lone flight of Canada geese; / and blew back the low, inaudible rollers / in upright, steely mist."

ELIZABETH BISHOP
"The End of March" from THE COMPLETE BOOK OF POEMS 1927–1979

"Highways and cross-paths are hastily traversed; and, clambering down a crag, I find myself at the extremity of a long beach. How gladly does the spirit leap forth, and suddenly enlarge its sense of being to the full extent of the broad, blue, sunny deep! A greeting and a homage to the Sea! I descend over its margin, and dip my hand into the wave that meets me, and bathe my brow. That far-resounding roar is the Ocean's voice of welcome. His salt breath brings a blessing along with it. Now let us pace together—the reader's fancy arm in arm with mine—this noble beach."

NATHANIEL HAWTHORNE
"FOOT-PRINTS ON THE SEA-SHORE"

"I walk unseen / On the dry smooth-shaven green, / To behold the wandering moon, / Riding near her highest noon, / Like one that had been led astray / Through the heav'n's wide pathless way, / And oft, as if her head she bow'd, / Stooping through a fleecy cloud."

JOHN MILTON
"IL PENSEROSO"

"And did those feet in ancient time / Walk upon England's mountains green?"

WILLIAM BLAKE

"Died some, pro patria, / non"dulce"non"et décor"... / walked eye-deed in hell / believing in old men's lies."

EZRA POUND
"HUGH SELWYN MAUBERLE. E.P. ODE POUR L'ELECTION DE SON SEPULCHRE"

"And hast thou walked about (how strange a story!) / In Thebes's streets three thousand years ago, / When the Memnonium was in all its glory?"

HORACE (HORATIO) SMITH
"ADDRESS TO THE MUMMY AT BELZONI'S EXHIBITION"

"When you intentionally walk at night, however, you encounter a cool blackness that blots out the visual scene and magnifies sound."

MARLYN S. DOAN
HIKING LIGHT

"If a walker is indeed an individualist there is nowhere he can't go at dawn and not many places he can't go at noon. But just as it demeans life to live alongside a great river you can no longer swim in or drink from, to be crowded into safer areas and hours takes much of the gloss off walking—one sport you shouldn't have to reserve a time and a court for."

EDWARD HOAGLAND
CITY WALKING

"The essence of this bliss was to walk by yourself in the black night; the slide shut, the top-coat buttoned; not a ray escaping, whether to conduct your footsteps or to make your glory public: a mere pillar of darkness in the dark; and all the while, deep down in the privacy of your fool's heart, to know you had a bull's-eye at your belt, and to exult and sing over the knowledge."

ROBERT LOUIS STEVENSON
THE LANTERN-BEARERS

"It is nearly five o'clock when I start walking. The afternoon is brilliant and warm, absolutely still, not enough air stirring to move a leaf. There is only the steady somnolent trilling of insects, and now and again in the woods below me the cry of a pileated woodpecker."

WENDELL BERRY

"To him whose elastic and vigorous thought keeps pace with the sun, the day is a perpetual morning."

HENRY DAVID THOREAU

"... in winter the champagne brightness of the air and the sociability of the streets are grateful."

VIRGINIA WOOLF
"STREET HAUNTING"

"You cannot imagine what a nice walk we had round the orchard ... I hear today that an apricot has been detected on one of the trees."

JANE AUSTEN
LETTER, MAY 1808

"May you have warm words on a cool evening,
a full moon on a dark night,
and a smooth road all the way to your door."

IRISH TOAST

—————

"He found us a powerful young man, short sword on his hip and oak walking stick in hand, and off we went, not without a little trepidation. As forewarned, the mountain was steep, the trail narrow, not even a birdcall to be heard. We made our way through deep forest dark as night, reminding me of Tu Fu's poem about 'clouds bringing darkness.' We groped through thick bamboo, waded streams, climbed through rocks, sweaty, fearful, and tired, until we finally came to the village of Mogami. Our guide, turning back, said again how the trail was tough."

MATSUO BASHO
"THE NARROW ROAD TO THE INTERIOR"

"I, who cannot stay in my chamber for a single day without acquiring some rust, and when sometimes I have stolen forth for a walk at the eleventh hour of four o'clock in the afternoon, too late to redeem the day, when the shades of night were already beginning to be mingled with the daylight, have felt as if I had committed some sin to be atoned for."

HENRY DAVID THOREAU
"WALKING"

"To enter out into that silence that was the city at eight o'clock of a misty evening in November, to put your feet upon that buckling concrete walk, to step over grassy seams and make your way, hands in pockets, through the silences, that was what Mr. Leonard Mead most dearly loved to do. He would stand upon the corner of an intersection and peer down long moonlit avenues of sidewalk in four directions, deciding which way to go, but it really made no difference; he was alone in this world of 2052 A.D. or as good as alone, and with a final decision made, a path selected, he would stride off, sending patterns of frosty air before him like the smoke of a cigar. . . ."

RAY BRADBURY
PEDESTRIAN

"I was walking in a dark valley / and above me the tops of the hills / had caught the morning light."

WENDELL BERRY
"RETURNING" FROM *THE WHEEL*

"Where the fair columns of St. Clement stand, / Whose straiten'd bounds encroach upon the Strand; / Where the low penthouse bows the walker's head, / And the rough pavement wounds the yielding tread,"

JOHN GAY
"TRIVIA; OR, THE ART OF WALKING THE STREETS OF LONDON"

"The tent flaps in the warm / Early sun: I've eaten breakfast and I'll / take a walk / To Benson Lake. Packed a lunch, / Goodbye."

GARY SNYDER
"A WALK"

———•••••———

"Out walking in the frozen swamp one grey day / I paused and said, 'I will turn back from here. No, I will go on farther-and we shall see.'"

ROBERT FROST
"THE WOOD-PILE"

"It was December—a bright frozen day in the early morning. Far out in the country there was an old Negro woman with her head tied red rag, coming along a path through the pinewoods. Her name was Phoenix Jackson. She was very old and small and she walked slowly in the dark pine shadows, moving a little from side to side in her steps, with the balanced heaviness and lightness of a pendulum in a grand-father clock."

EUDORA WELTY
A WORN PATH

"Every sunset which I witness inspires me with the desire to go to a West as distant and as fair as that into which the sun goes down."

HENRY DAVID THOREAU
"WALKING"

"Here when I walk the hutungs of a summer's evening as the moon rises over the city I can hear a lover's flute sending a tender message beyond the courtyard walls or the mournful monotony of a three-stringed lute."

HARRISON EVANS SALISBURY
"CAPTURING OLD ECHOES IN THE NEW PEKING," *NEW YORK TIMES*, FEBRUARY 10, 1985

"I sometimes go back to walk through the ghostly remains of Sutton Place where the rude, new buildings stand squarely in one another's river views."

JOHN CHEEVER
"MOVING OUT," *ESQUIRE*, JUNE 1983

"I am he that walks with the tender and growing night,"

WALT WHITMAN
LEAVES OF GRASS

"As I walked in, it got darker and denser; the birds began to screech and howler monkeys swung through the branches overhead. I worried about birds eyeing my white hair for nesting material (an oyster-catcher had done that in the Hebrides years ago); I wondered if vipers could be up among the monkeys. I'd watched *Nova*."

VIRGINIA BARTON BROWNBACK
"UNPAVED ROADS"

"And here we are again, a group of women hiking through the hills of Umbria, sipping wine, reading poetry under the starlit Umbrian sky, conquering the world."

PIER ROBERTS
"THE LUSHES"

"Details of the many walks I made along that crest have blurred, now, into a pleasing tapestry of grass and space and sunlight."

COLIN FLETCHER
THE SECRET WORLDS OF COLIN FLETCHER

"My walk was fine from place to place, / My jump was high on the top of the hill. / I had a great fondness for ships and boats / My heart was lively in my breast, / My feet as fleet as those of the hare, / Every muscle and joint like iron, / Good fortune confronted me everywhere / In the glen where I was reared."

DOUGLAS HYDE
"MY NATIVE GLEN"

"Ben Jonson exclaims—
'How near to good is what is fair!'
So I would say—
'How near to good is what is wild!'"

HENRY DAVID THOREAU
"WALKING"

"There are few greater delights than to walk up and down them in the evening alone with thousands of other people, up and down, relishing the lights coming through the trees or shining from the facades, listening to the sounds of music and foreign voices and traffic, enjoying the smell of flowers and good food and the air from the nearby sea. The sidewalks are lined with small shops, bars, stalls, dance halls, movies, booths lighted by acetylene lamps, and everywhere are strange faces, strange costumes, strange and delightful impressions. To walk up such a street into the quieter, more formal part of town, is to be part of a procession, part of a ceaseless ceremony of being initiated into the city and rededicating the city itself."

J. B. JACKSON
"THE STRANGER'S PATH"

Index